Festive Fall Coloring Book

By Matthew E. Breer

An adult coloring book, Inspired by Thanksgiving and the things of fall!

Over 40 illustrations for hours of stress relieving fun!

This book makes a perfect gift for everyone!

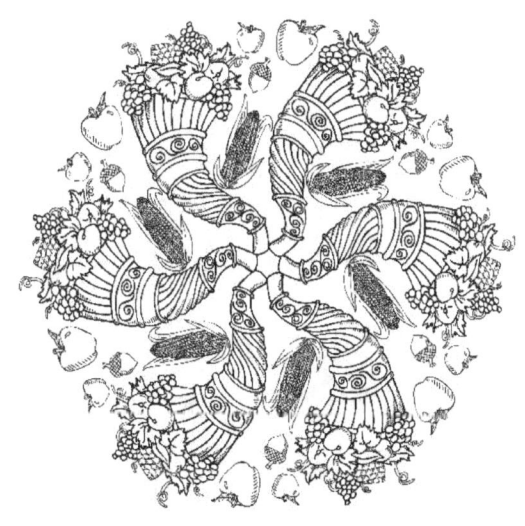

Be sure to check us out on Facebook and our website for other great things!

http://breerspublishing.weebly.com/

https://www.facebook.com/BreersPublishing/

Images in this book are created from public domain creative commons, royalty – free vintage art, and original art work. Copyright 2017 Breer's Art & Things Vintage publishing. All rights reserved.

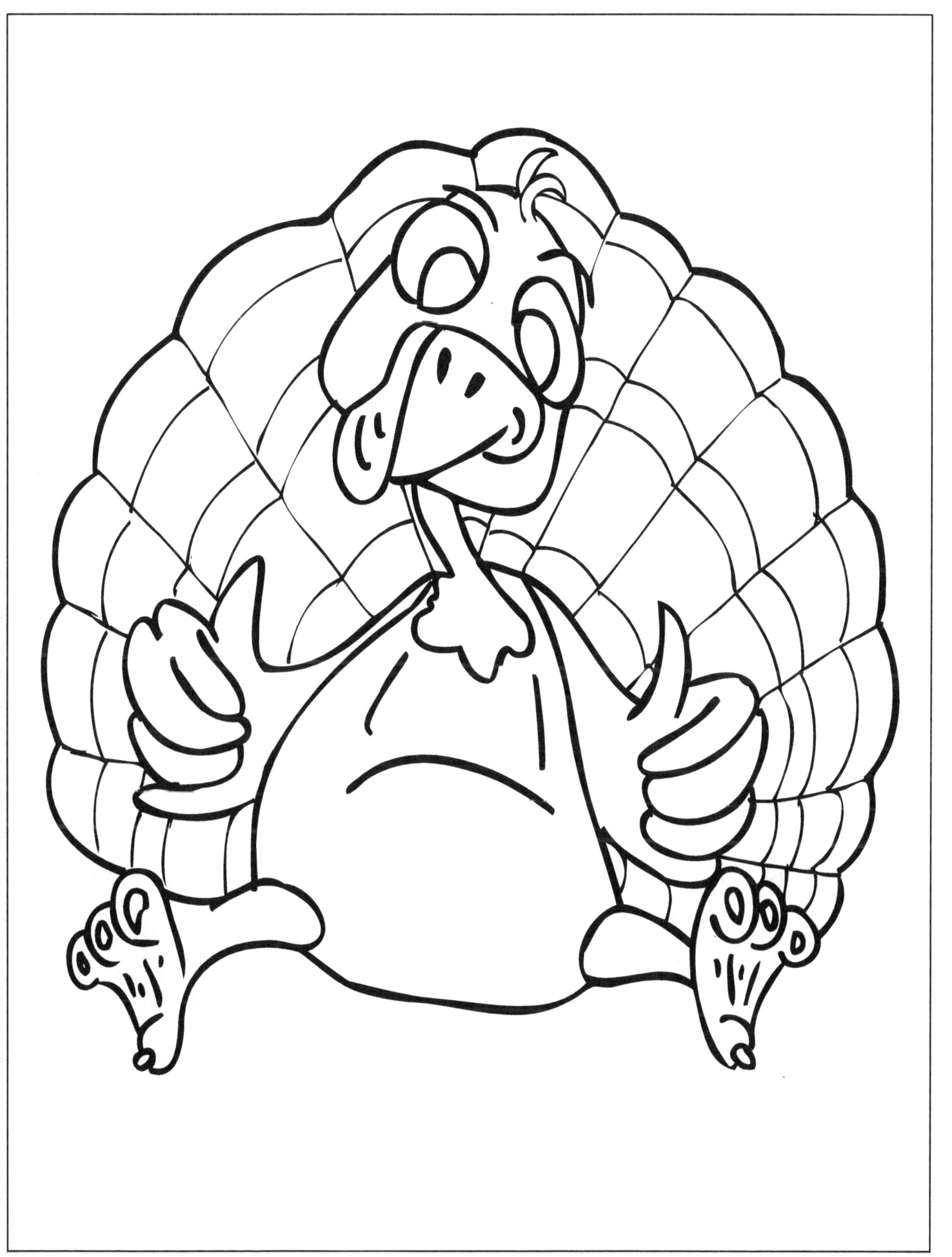

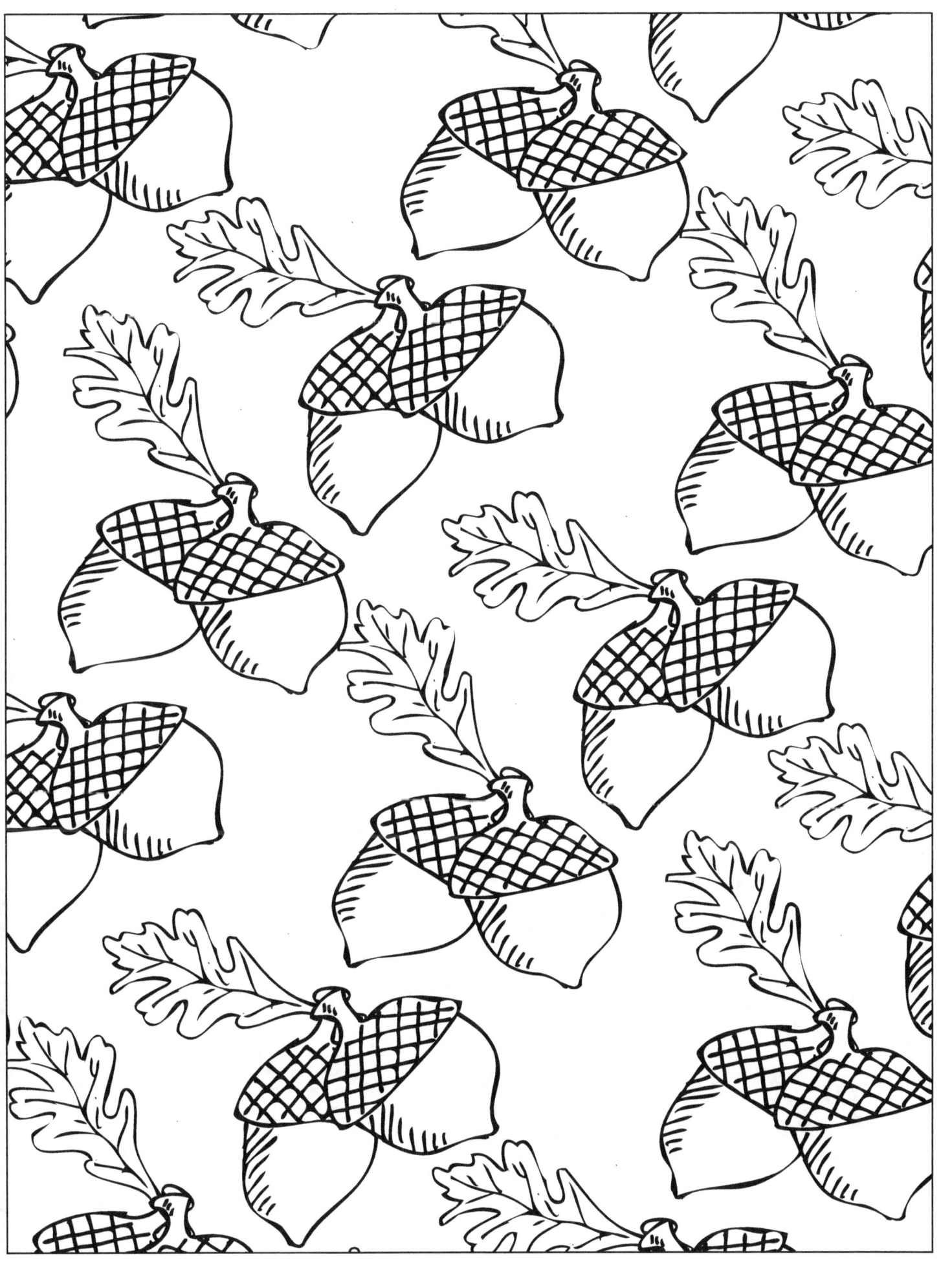

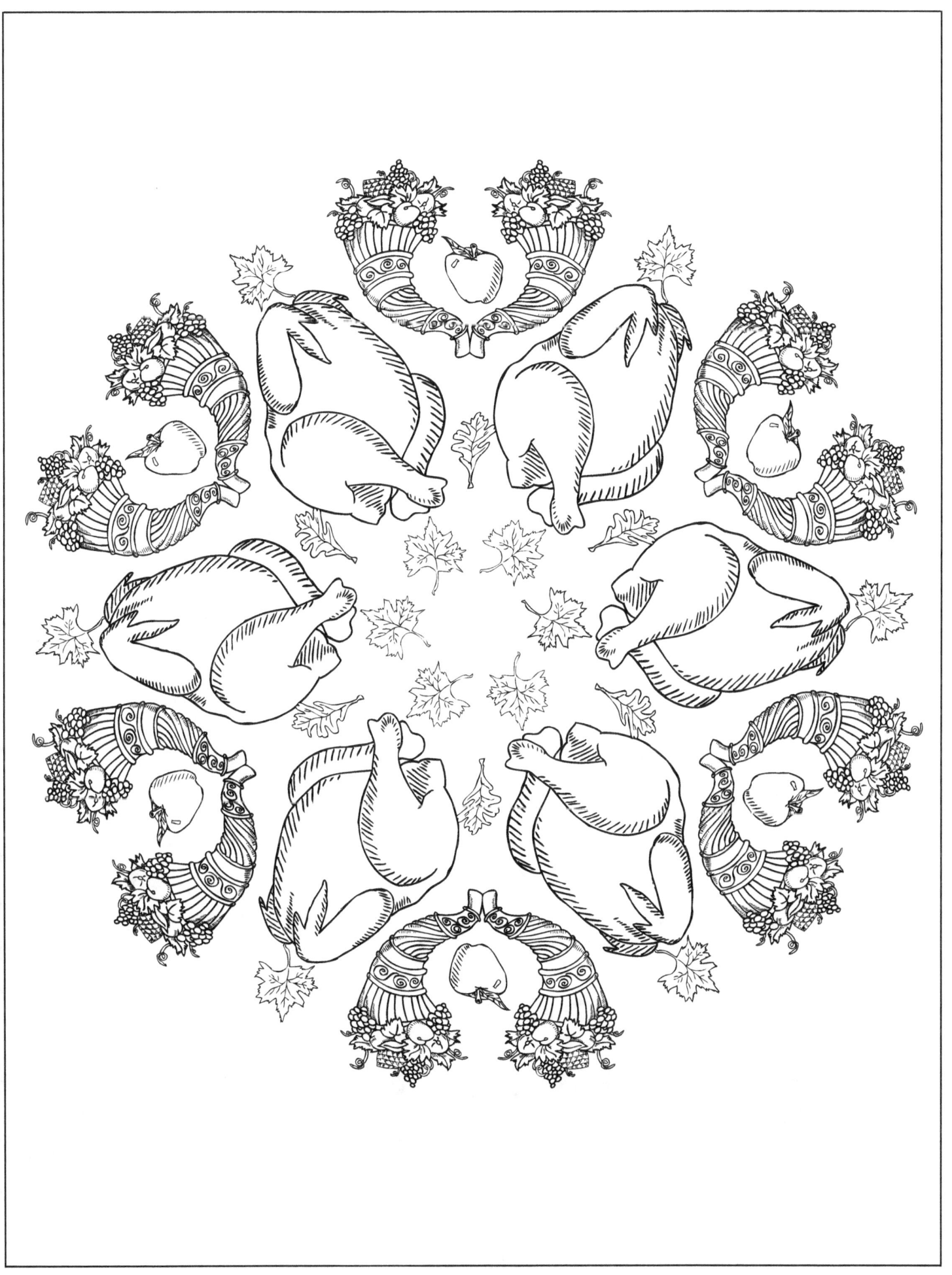

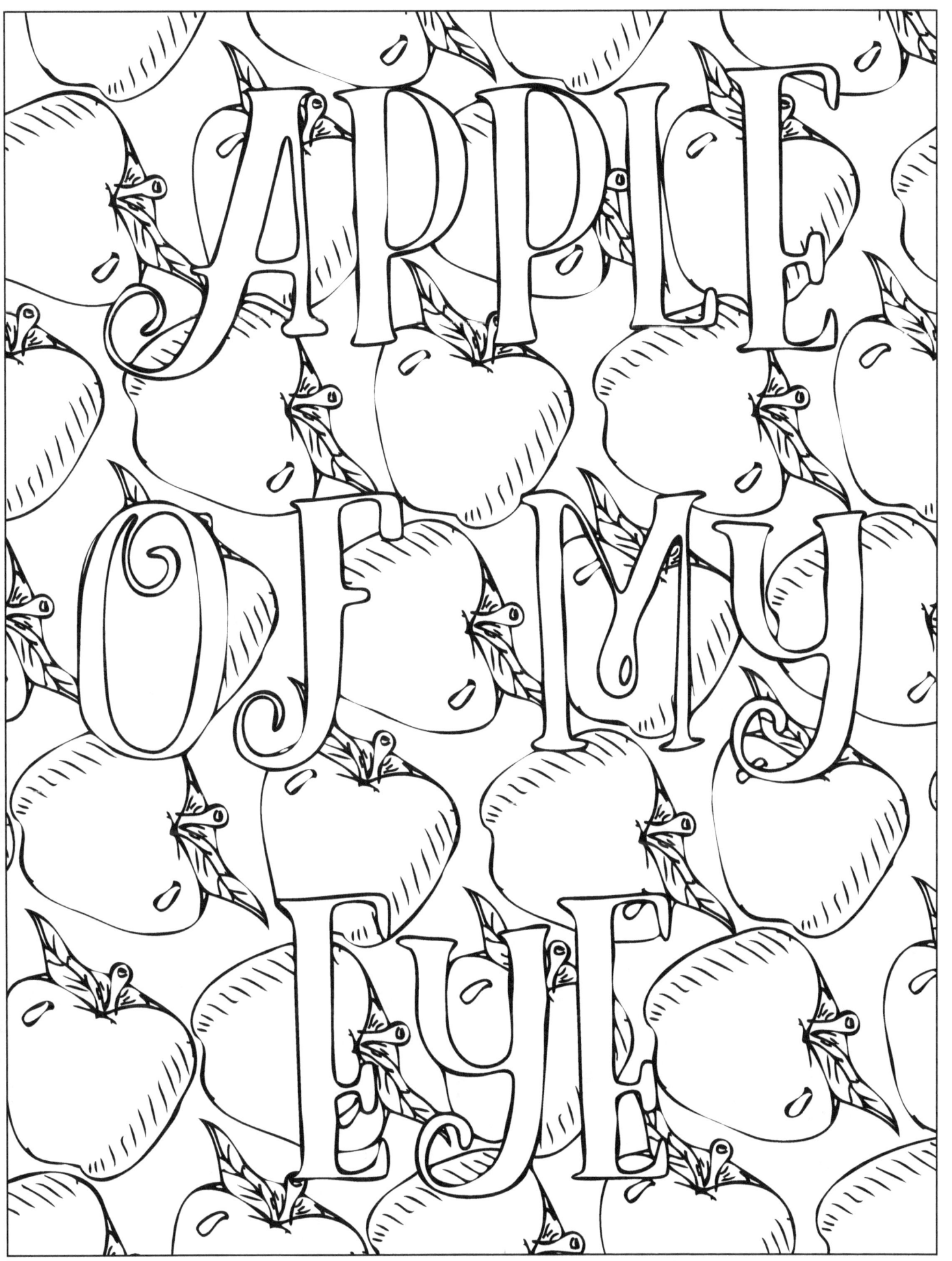

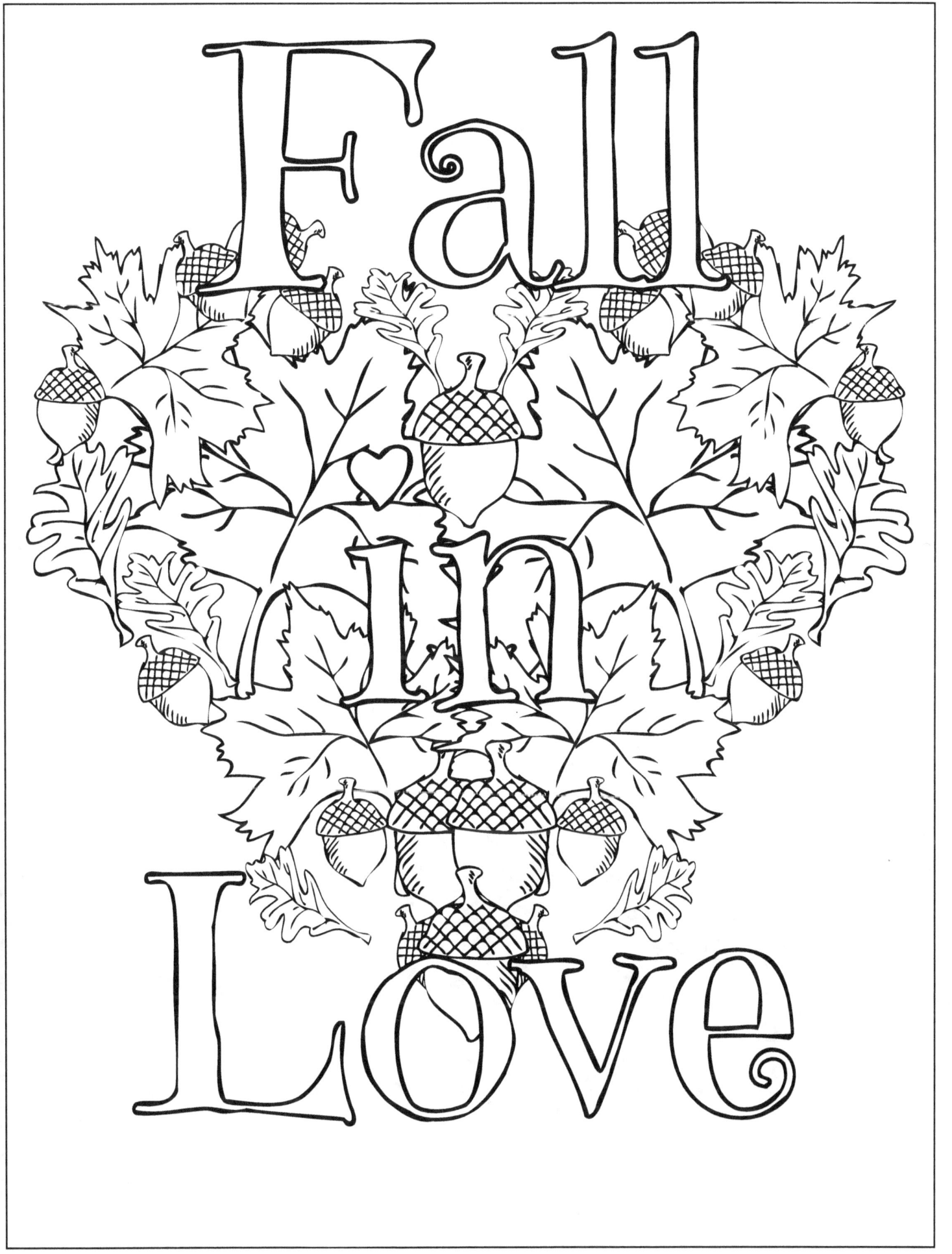

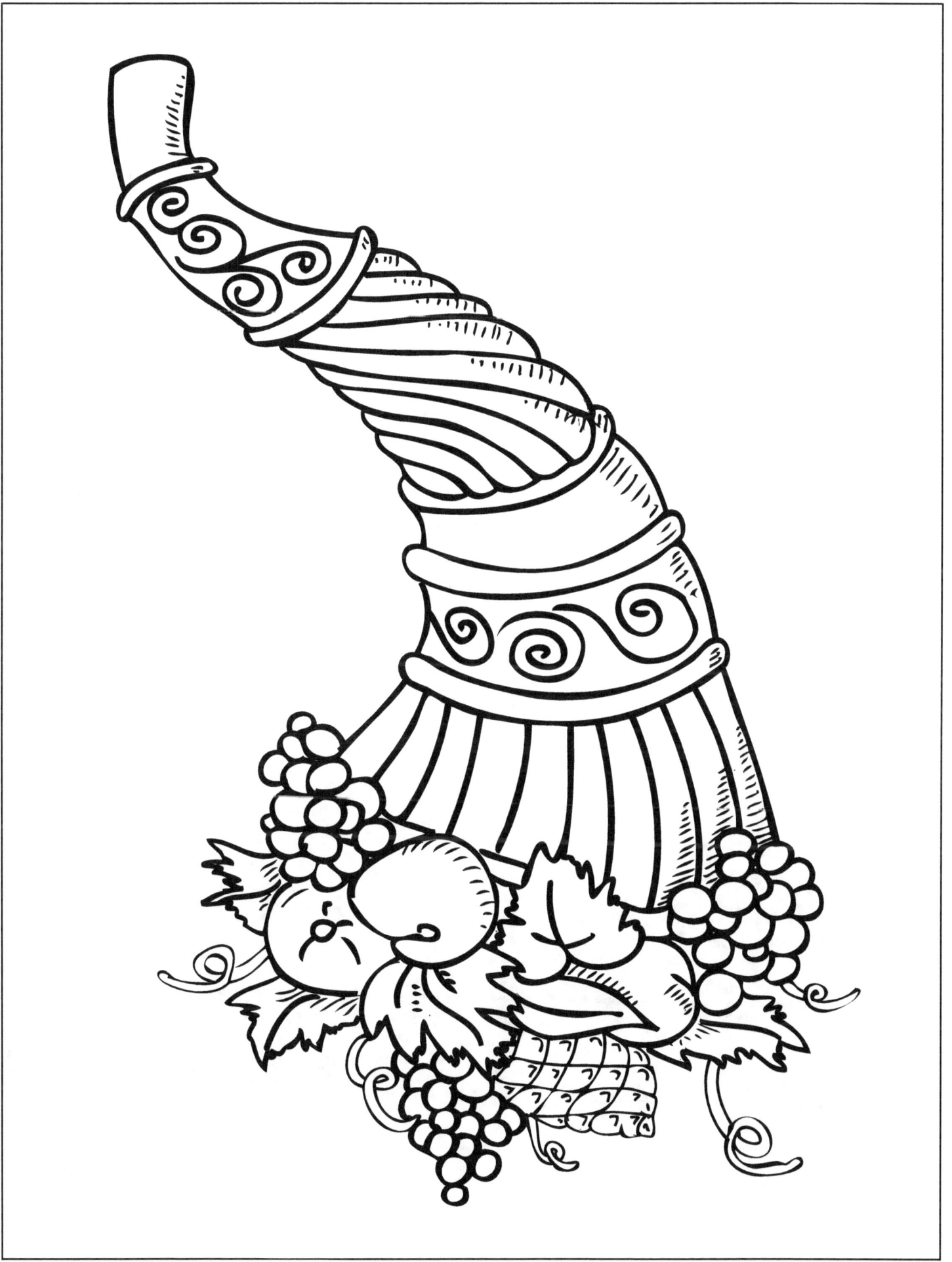

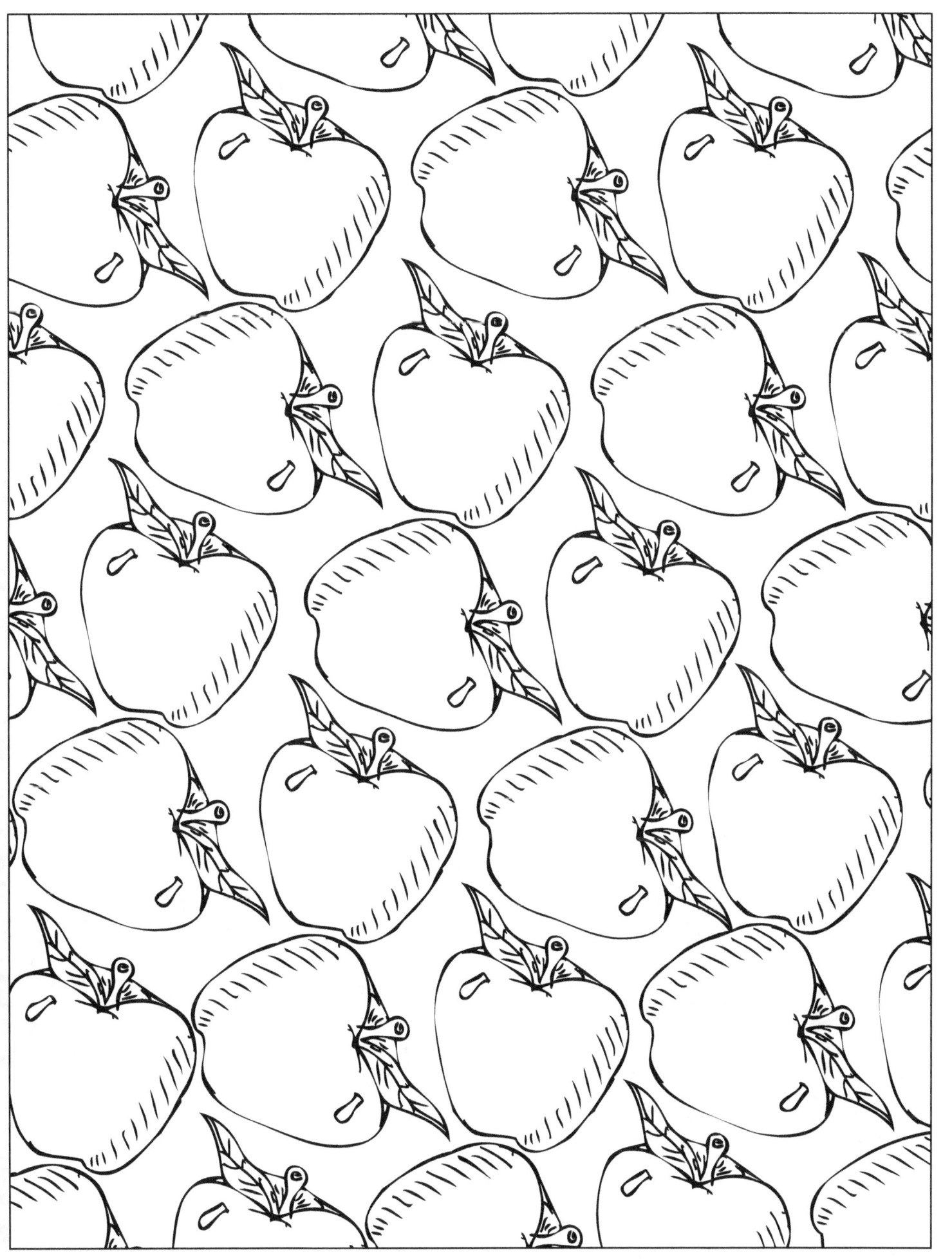

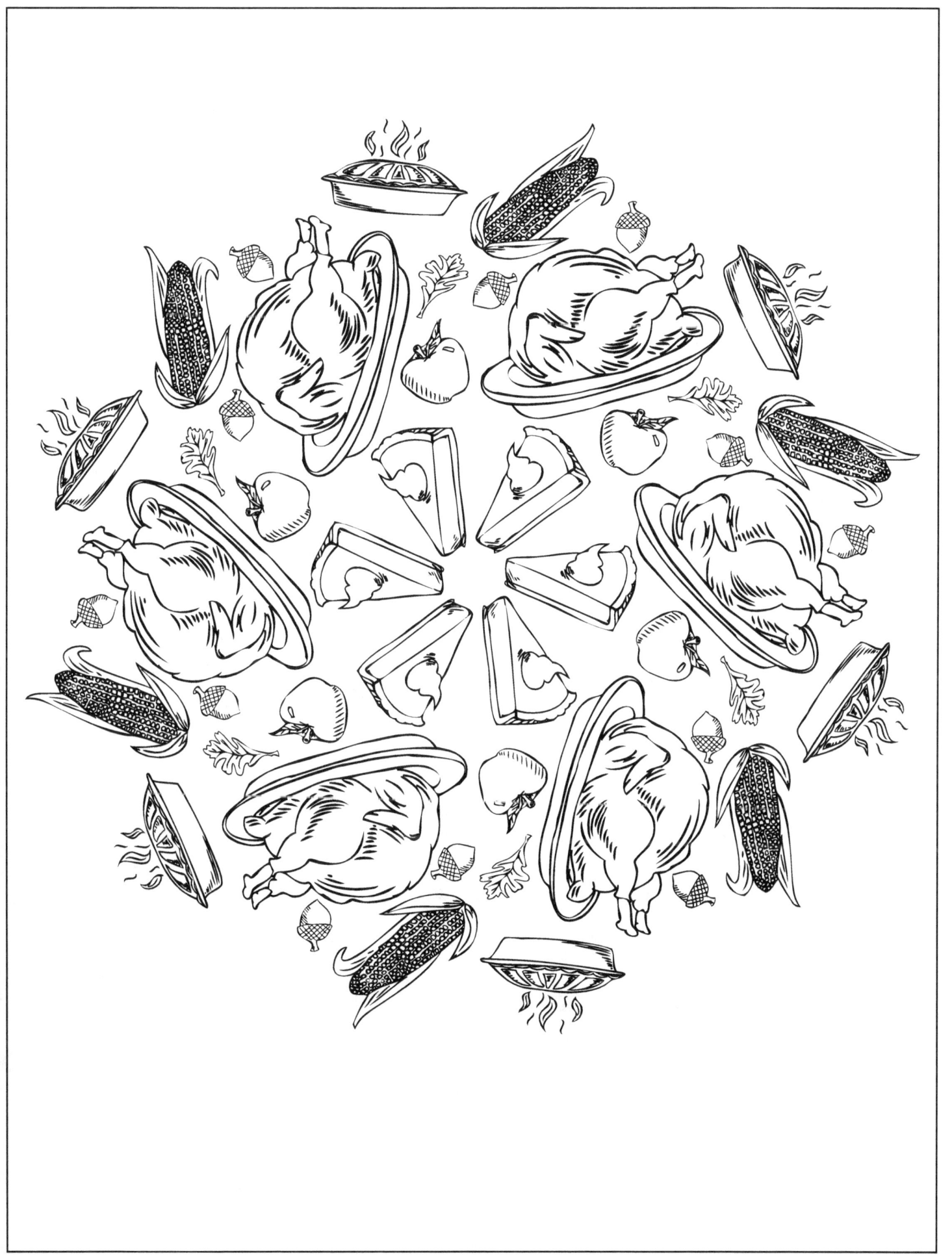

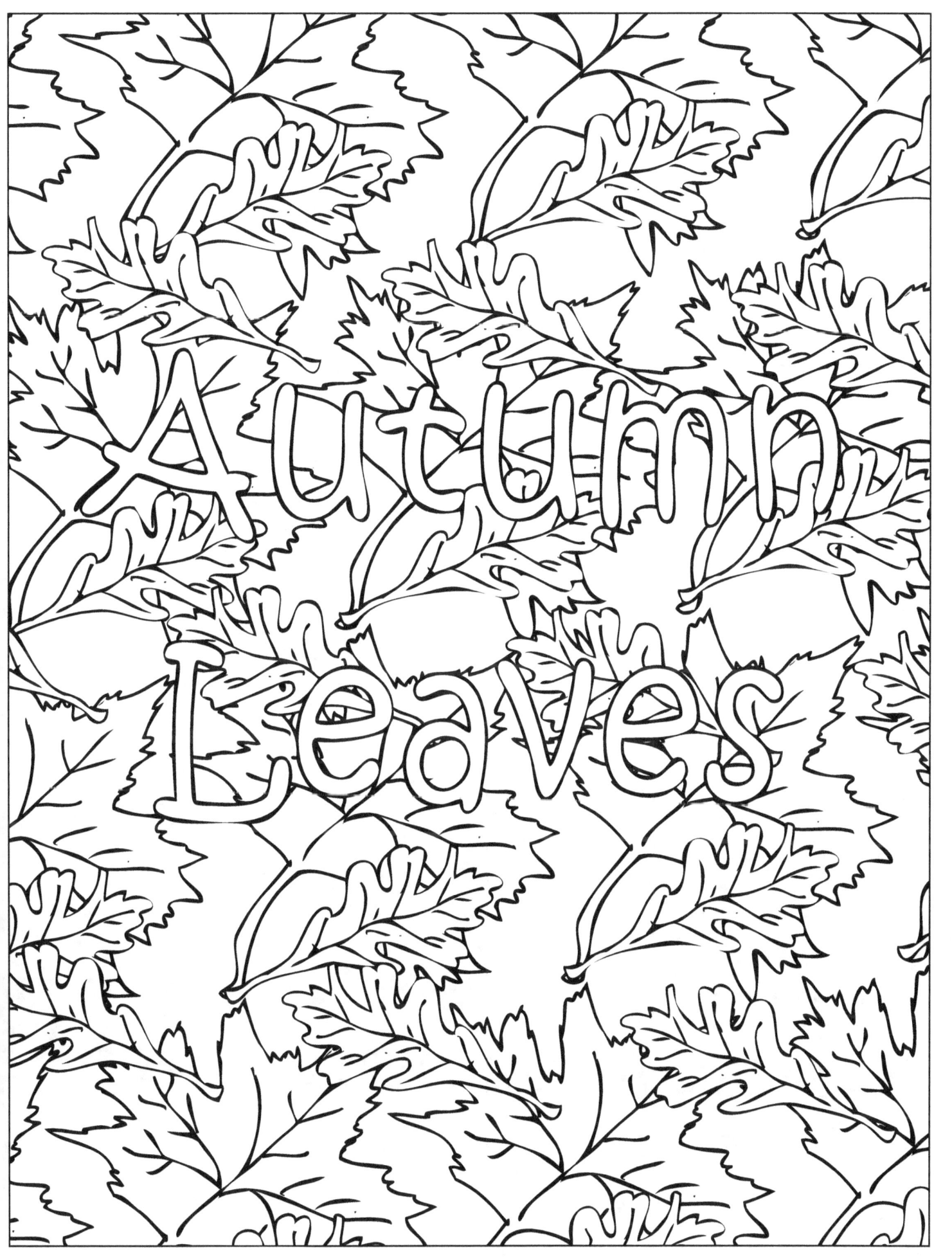

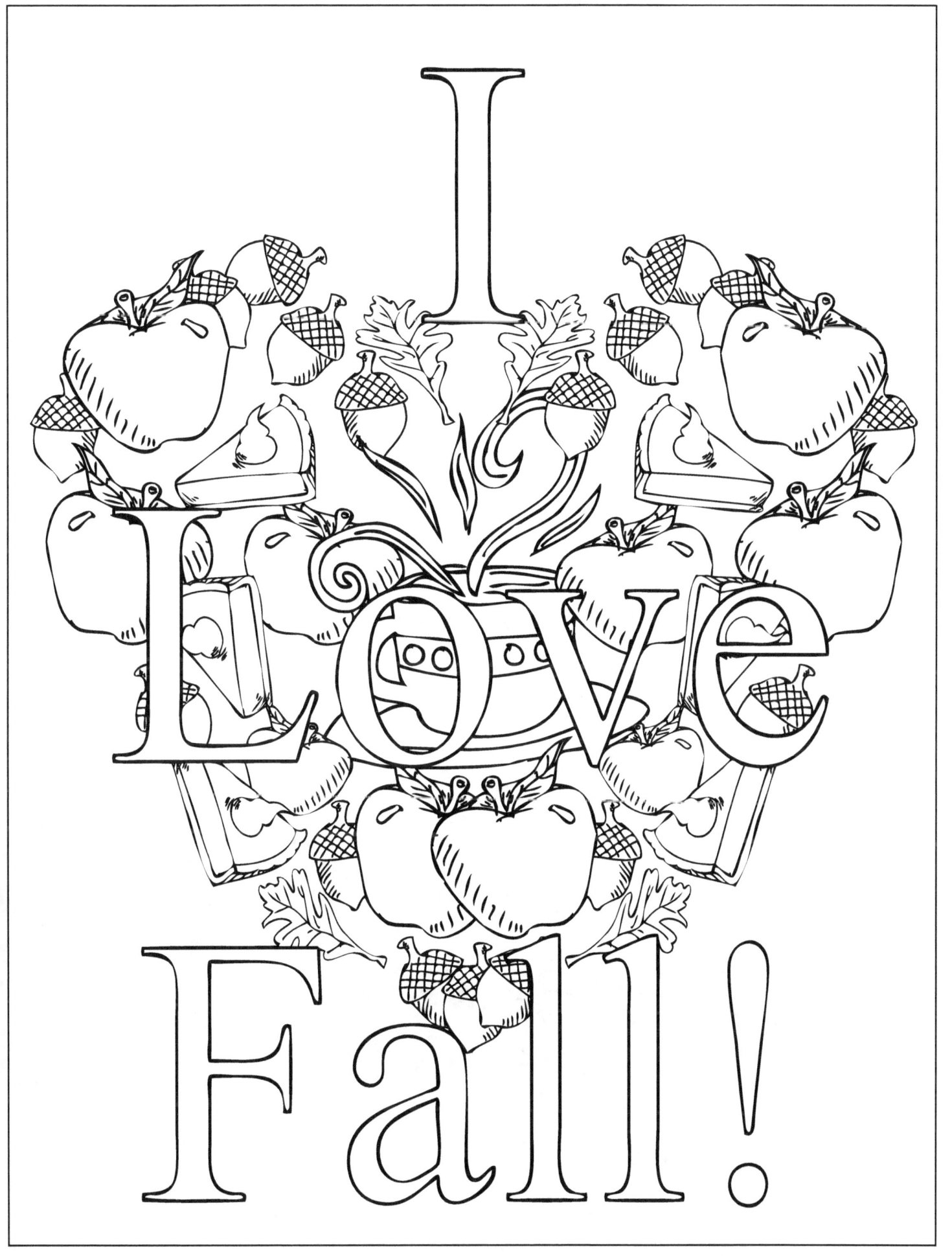

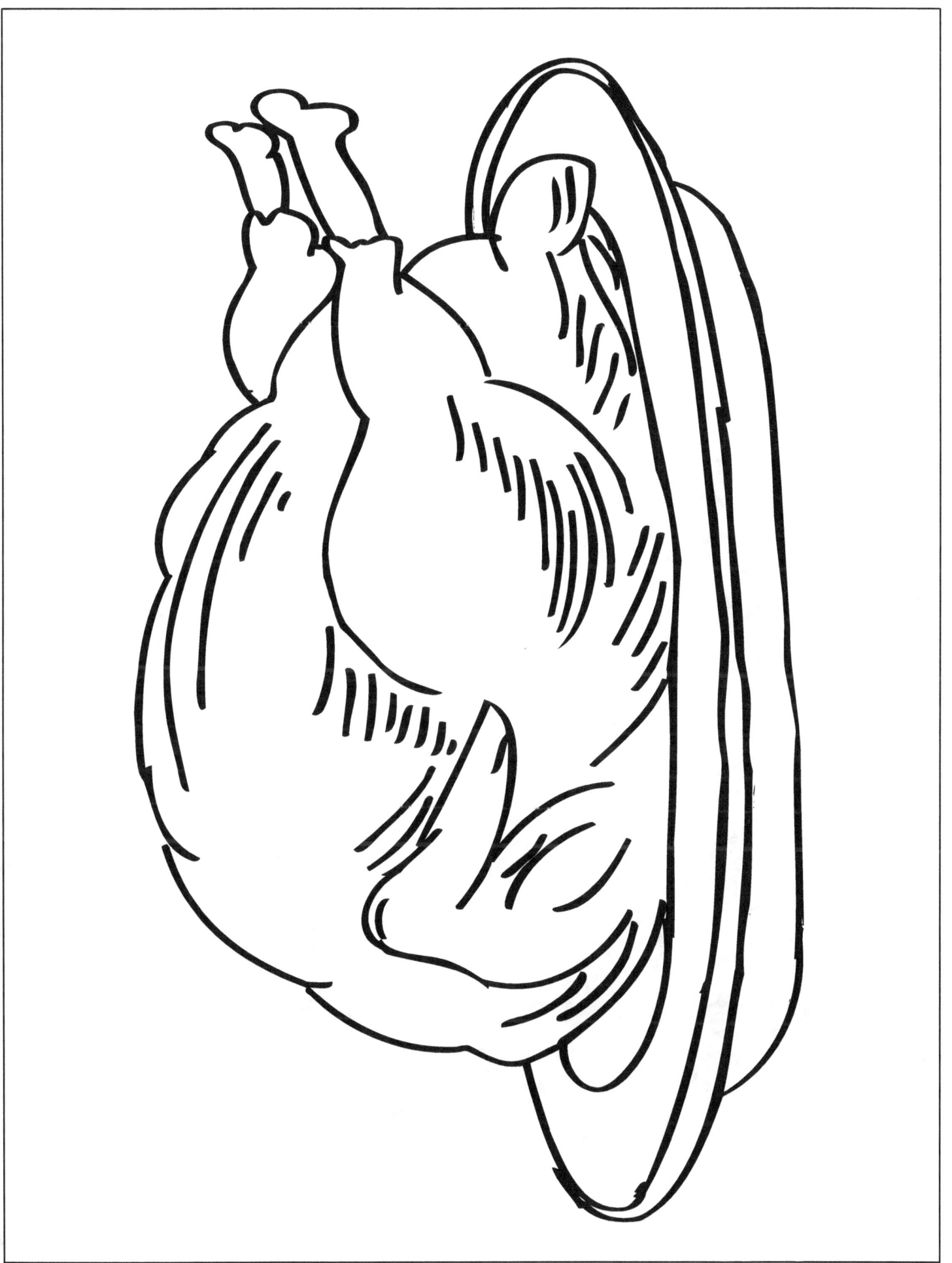

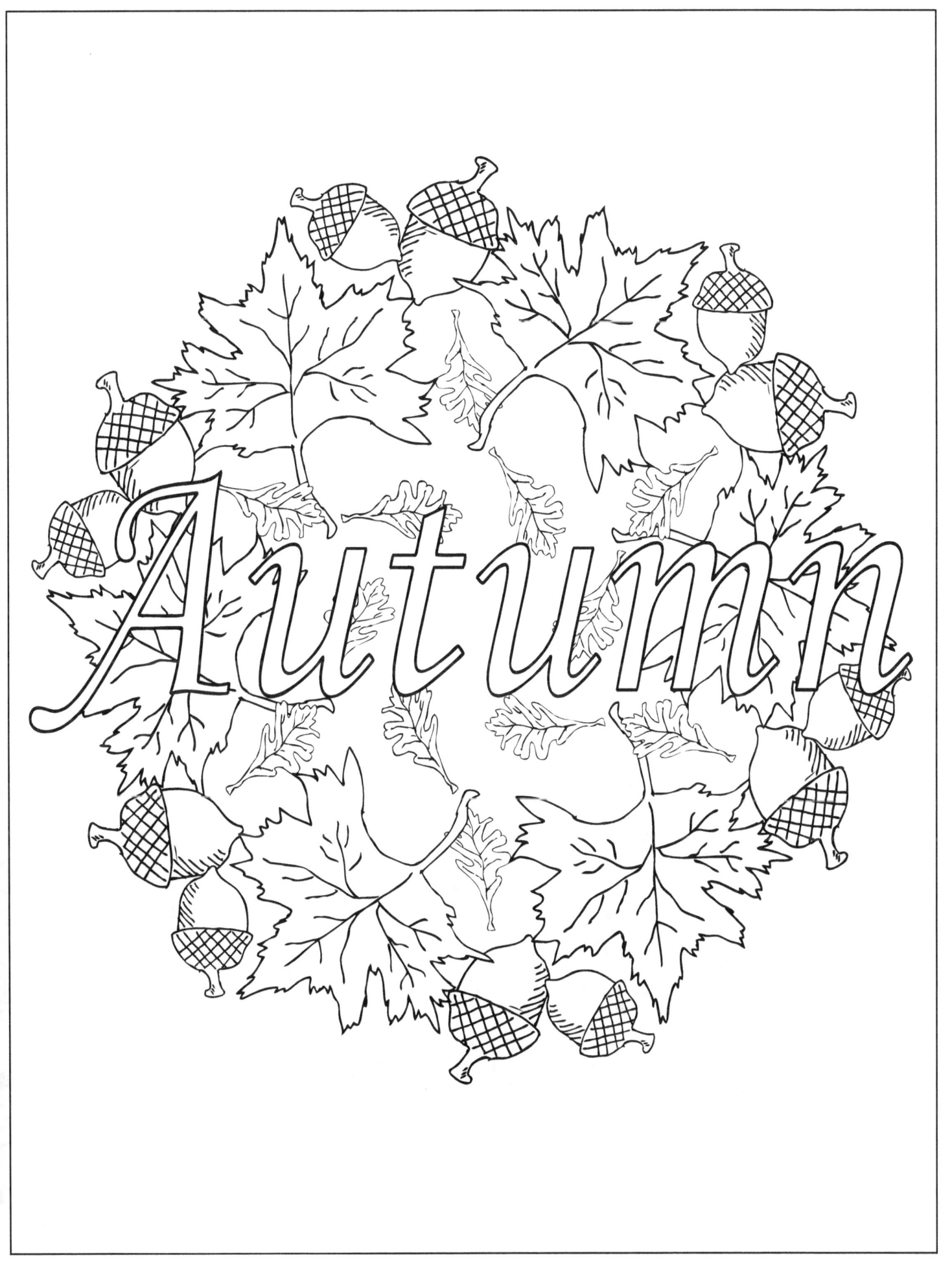

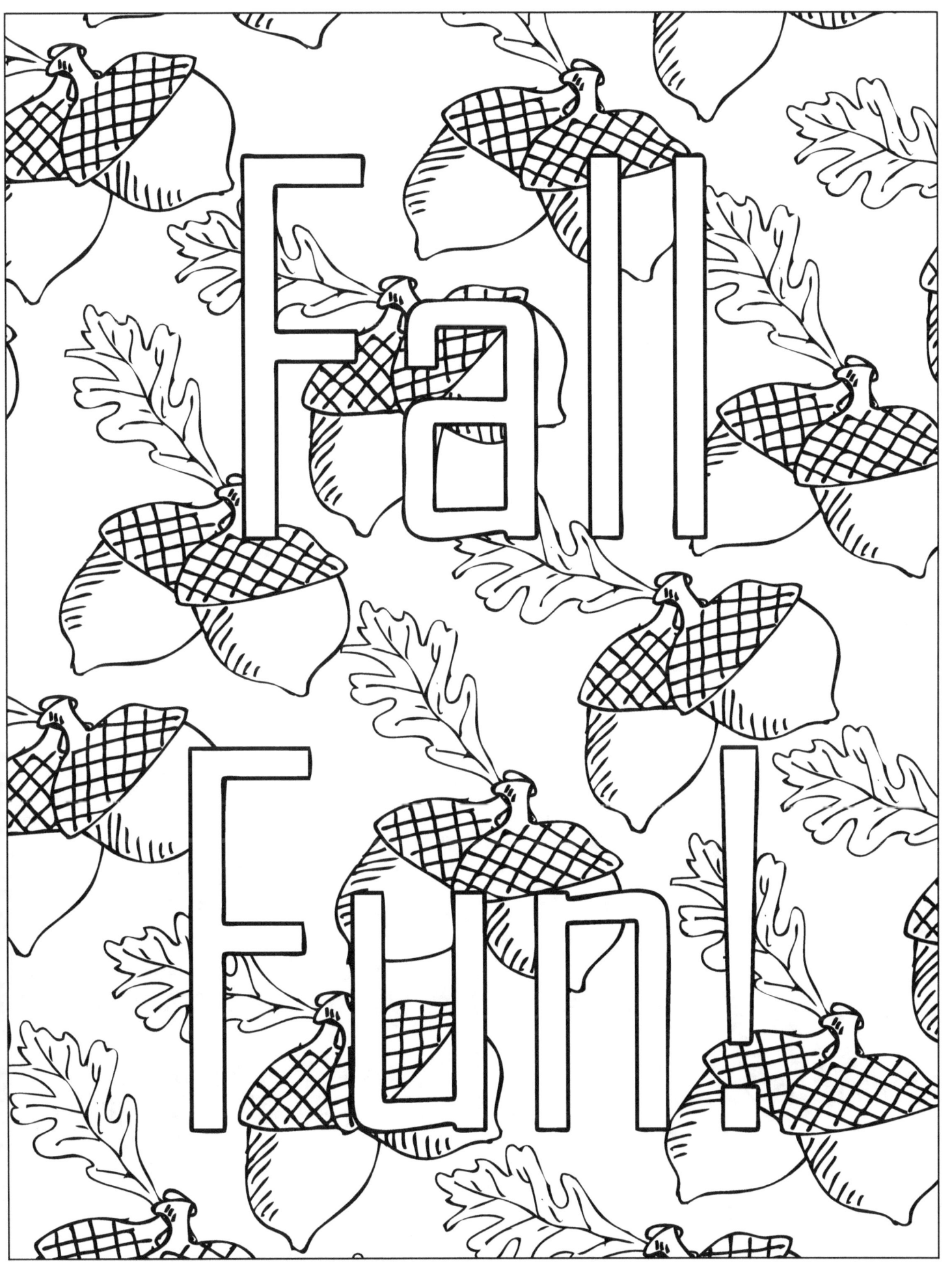

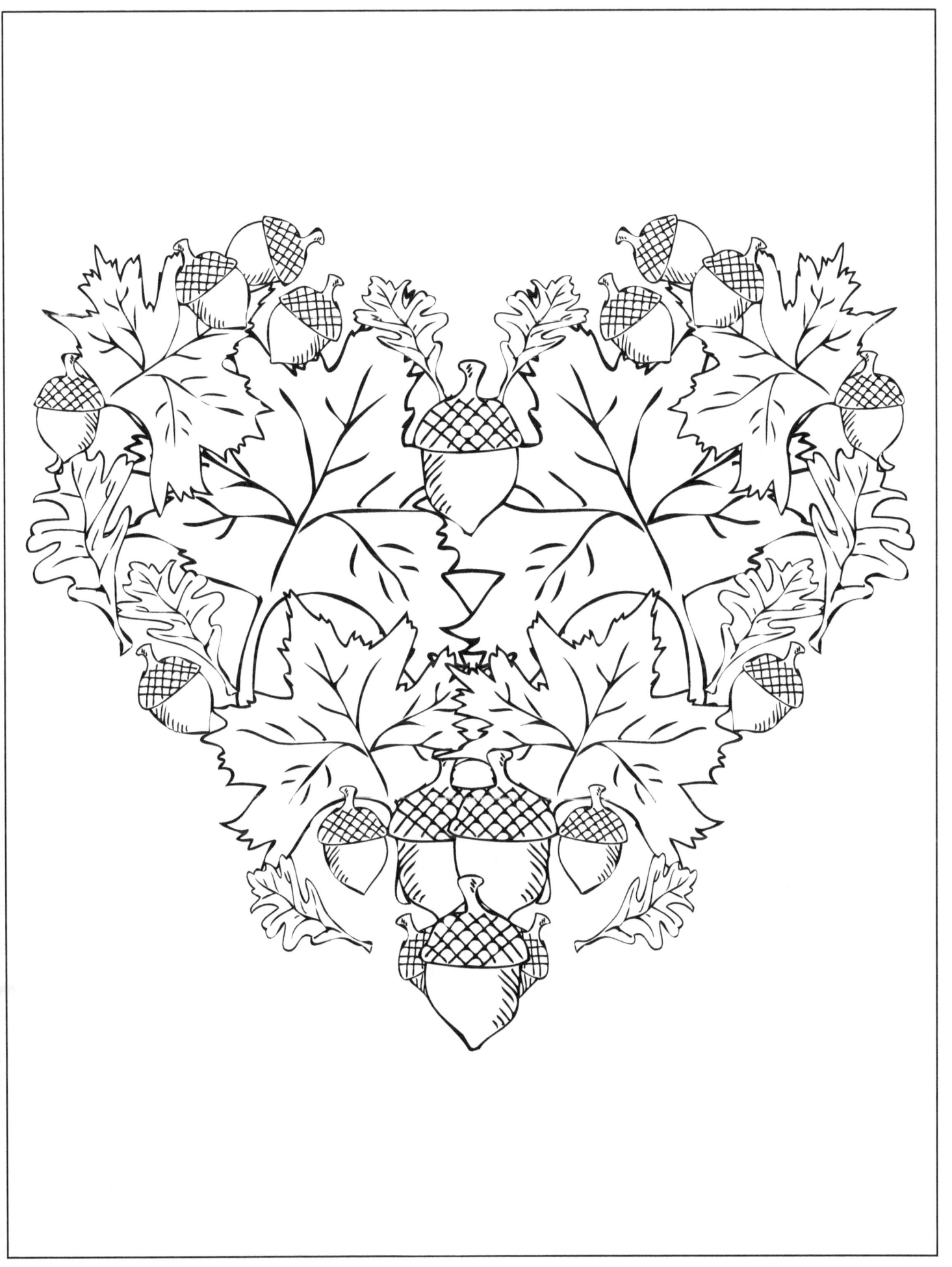

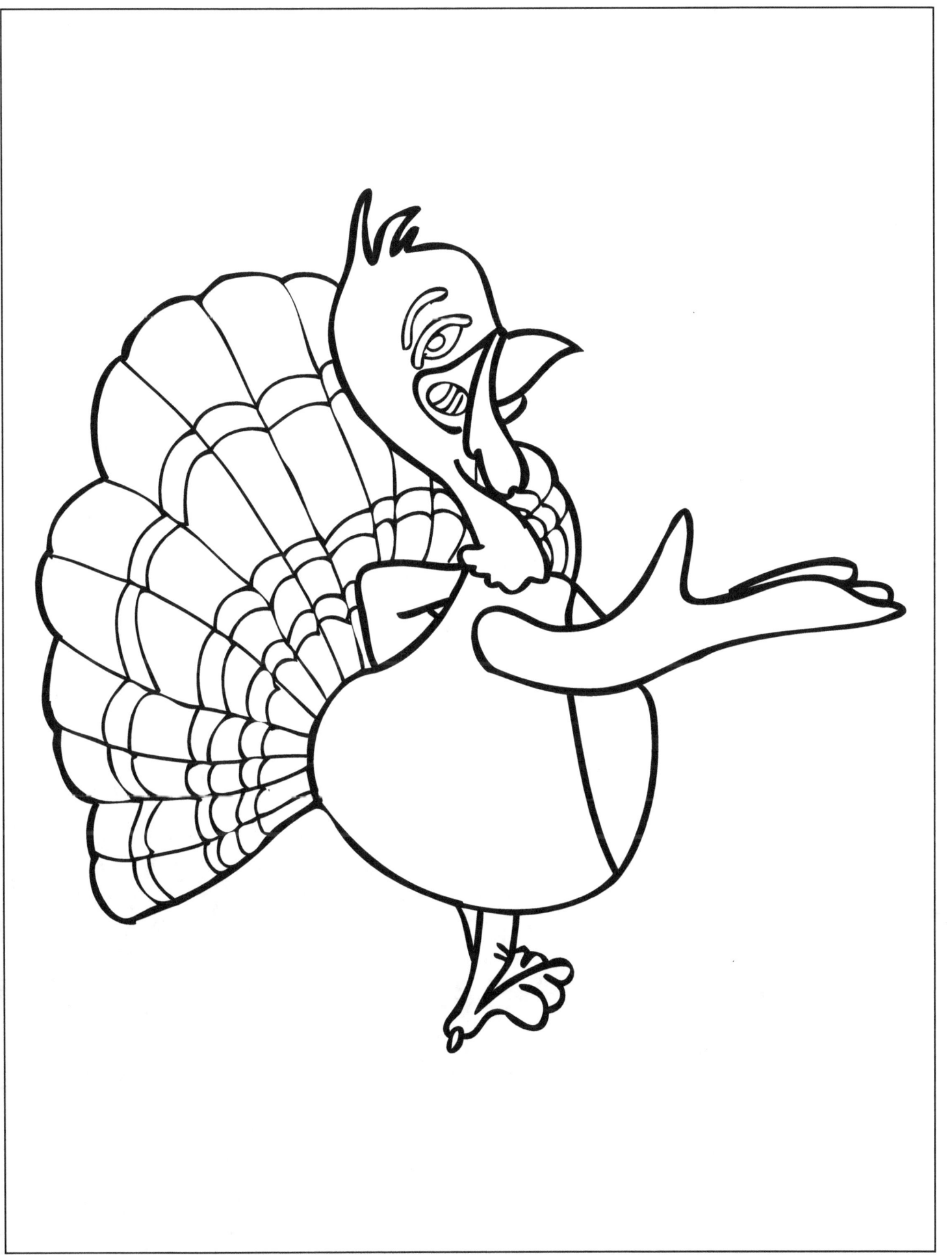

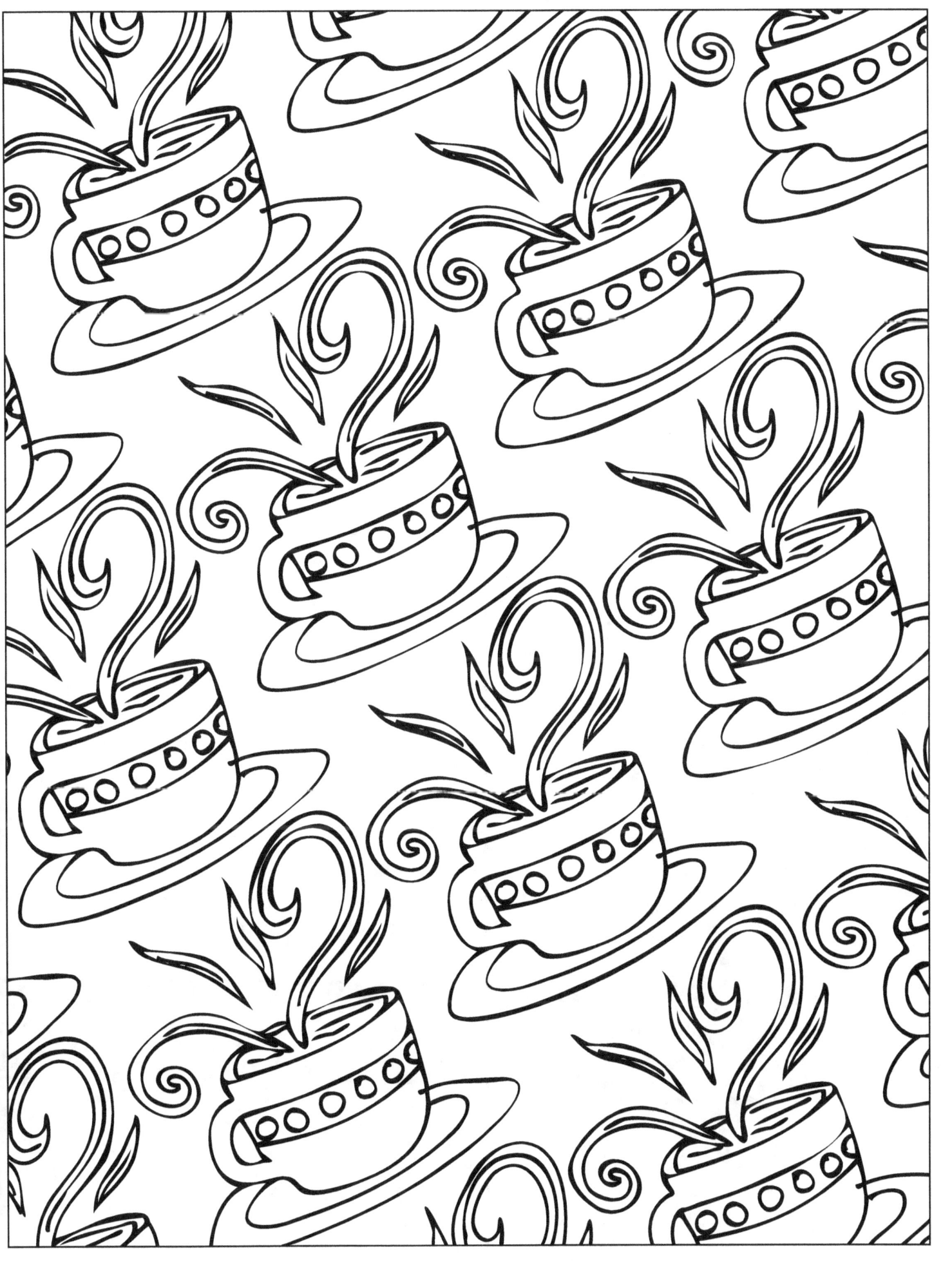

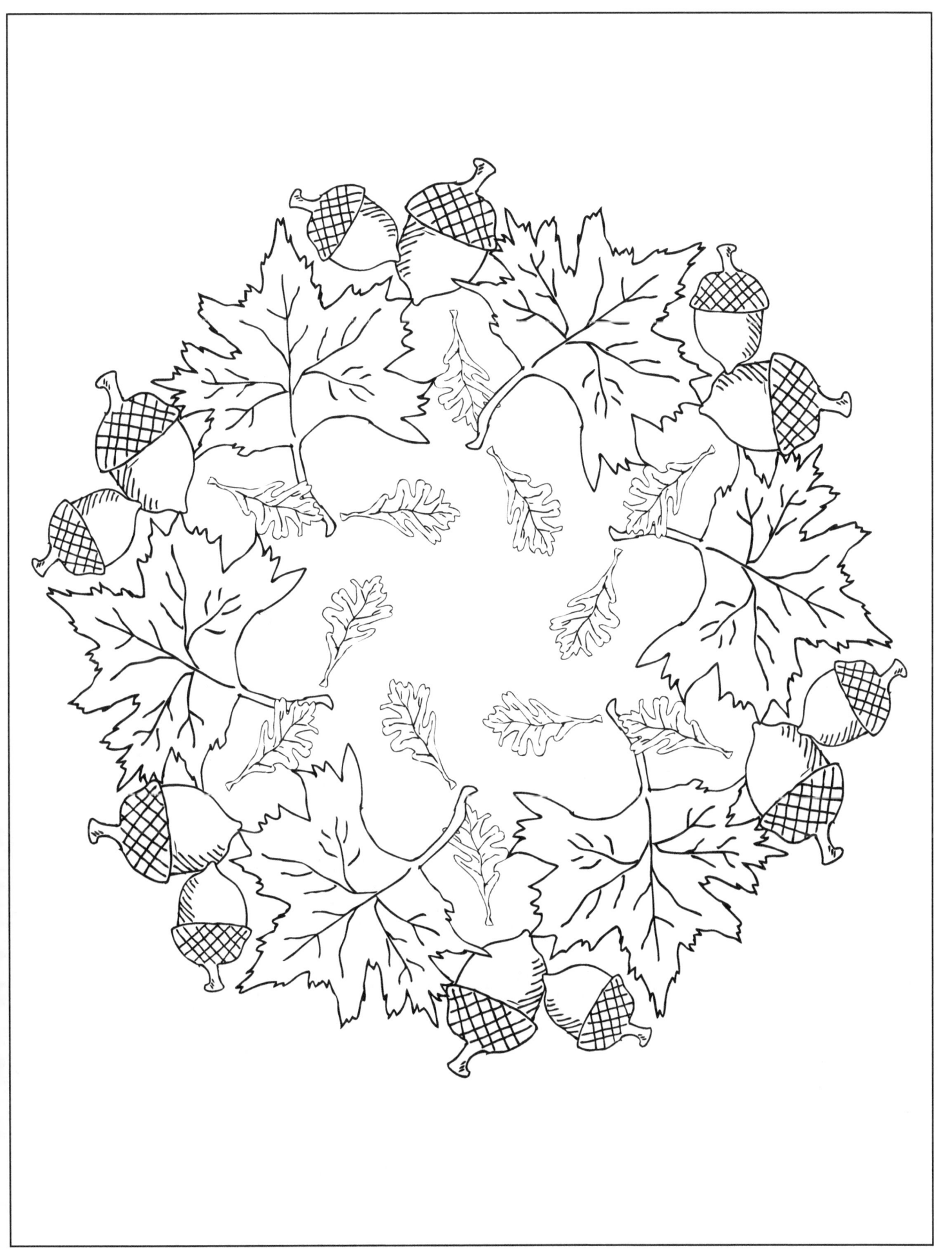

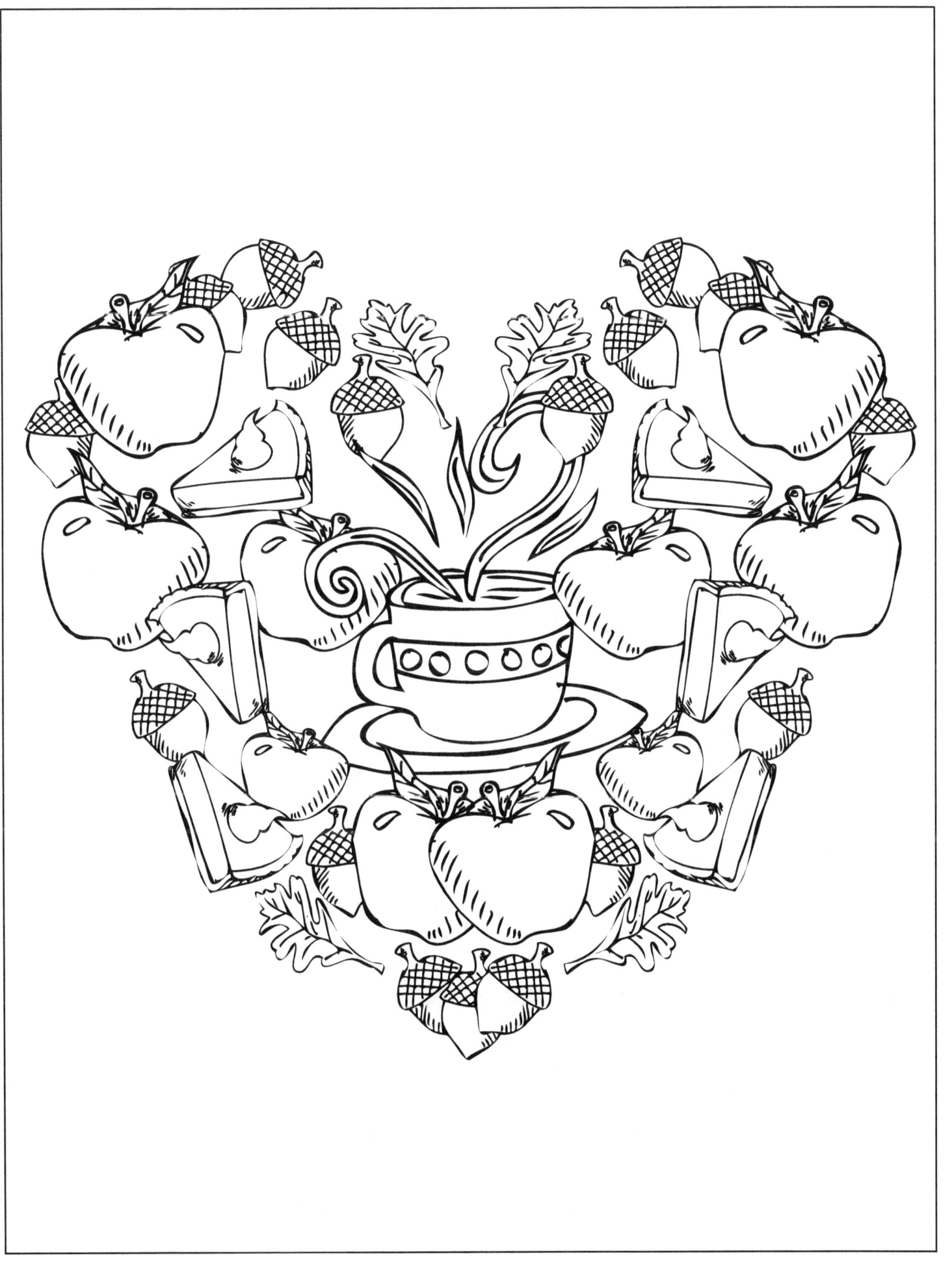

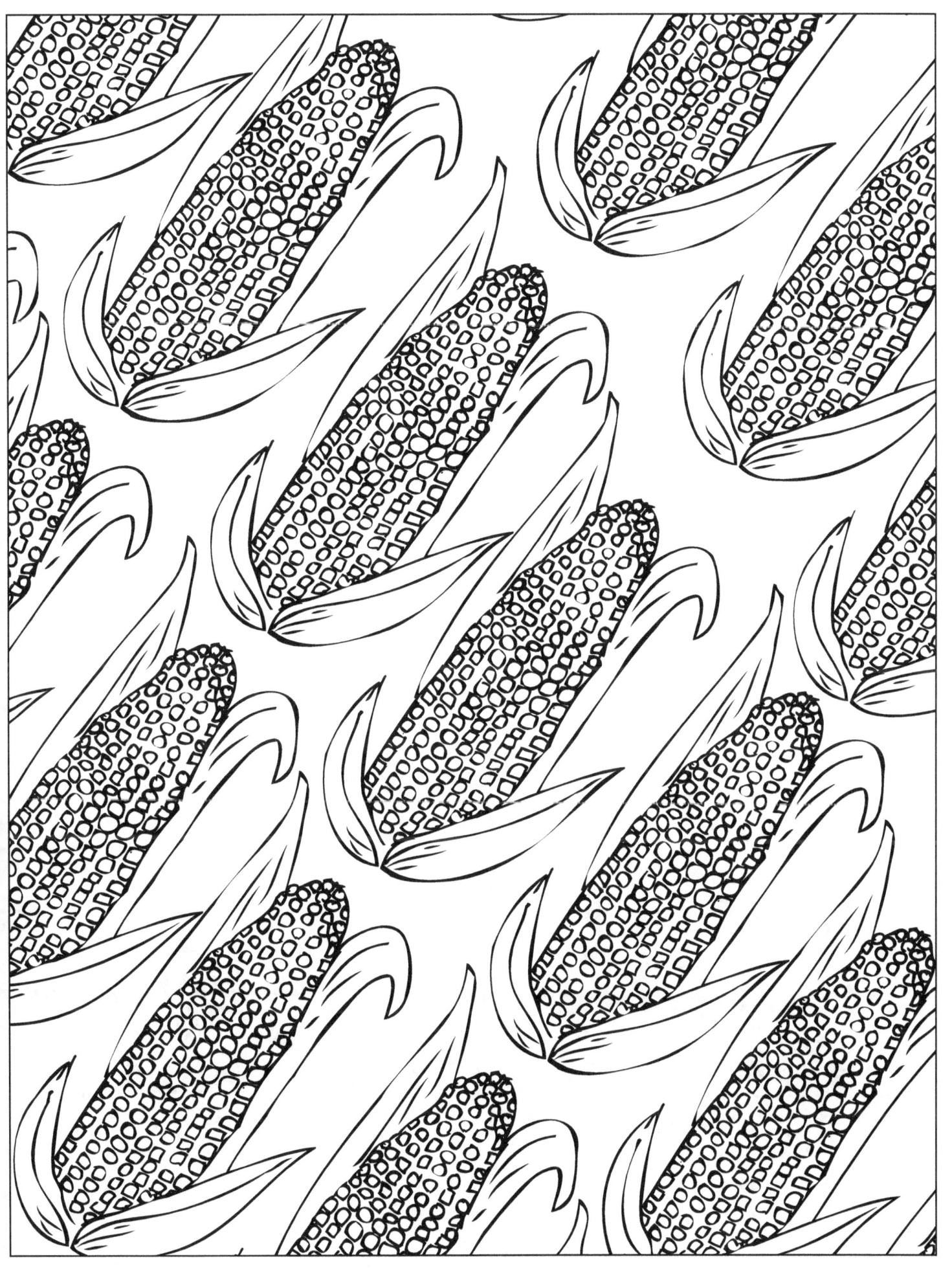

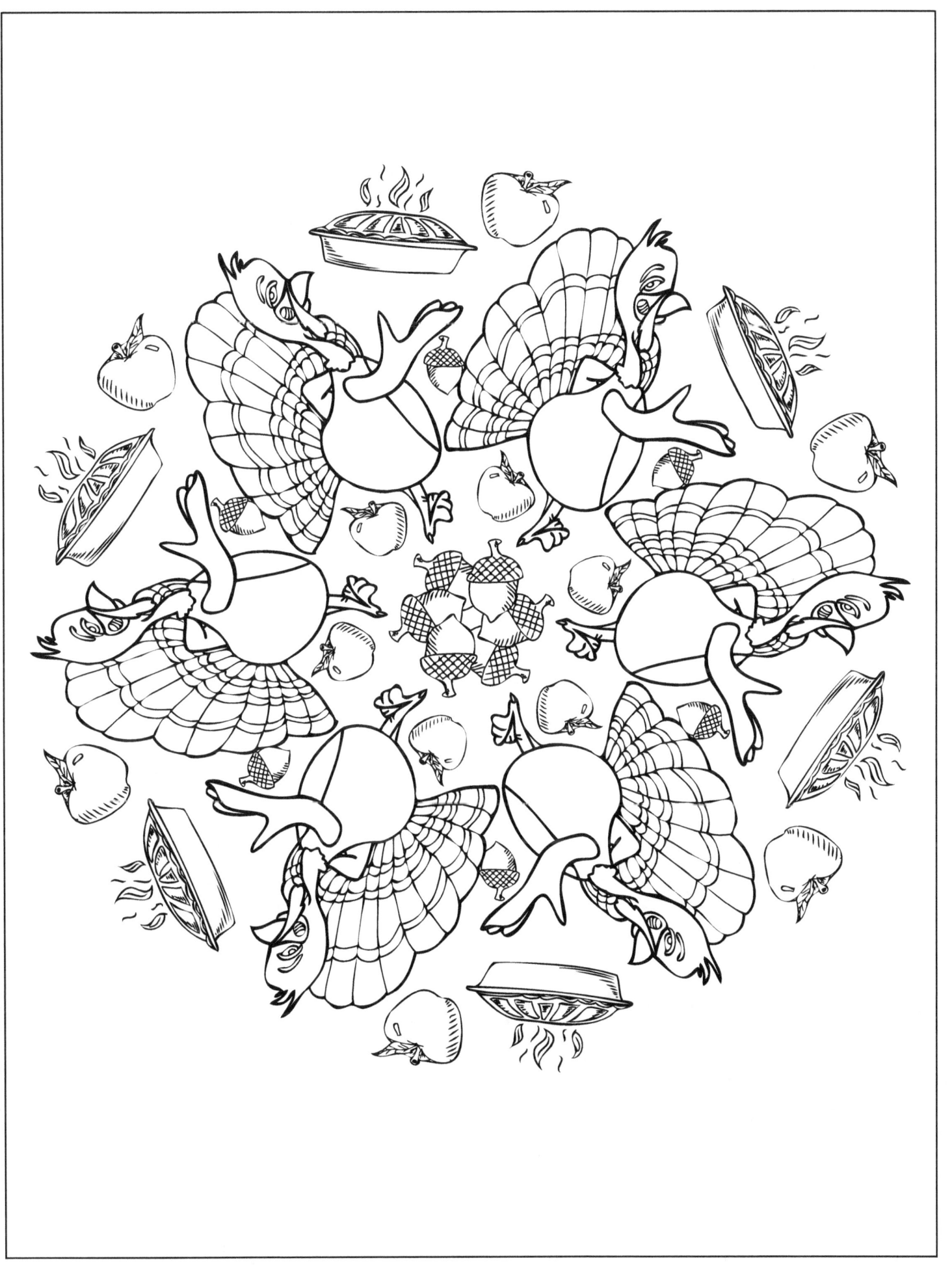

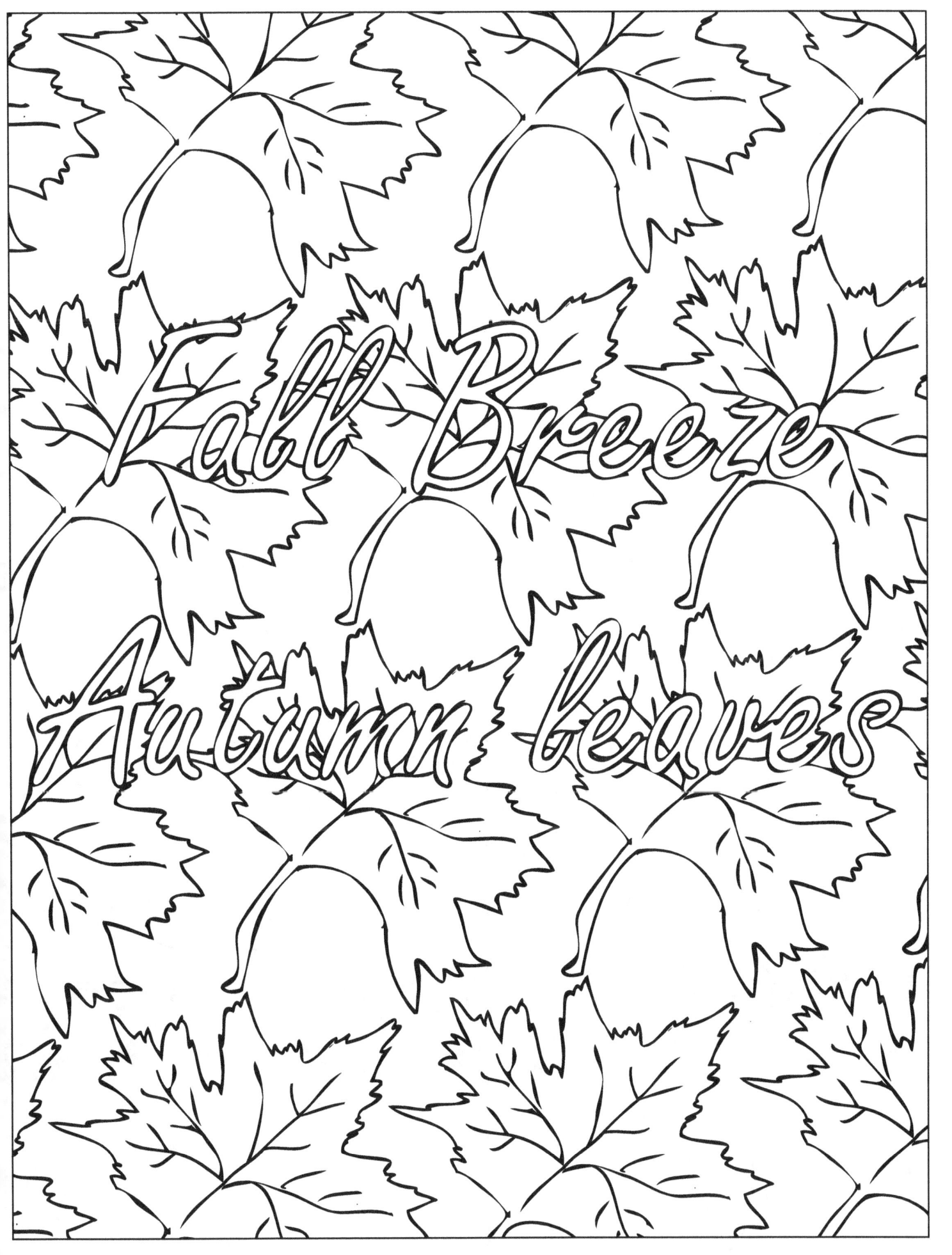

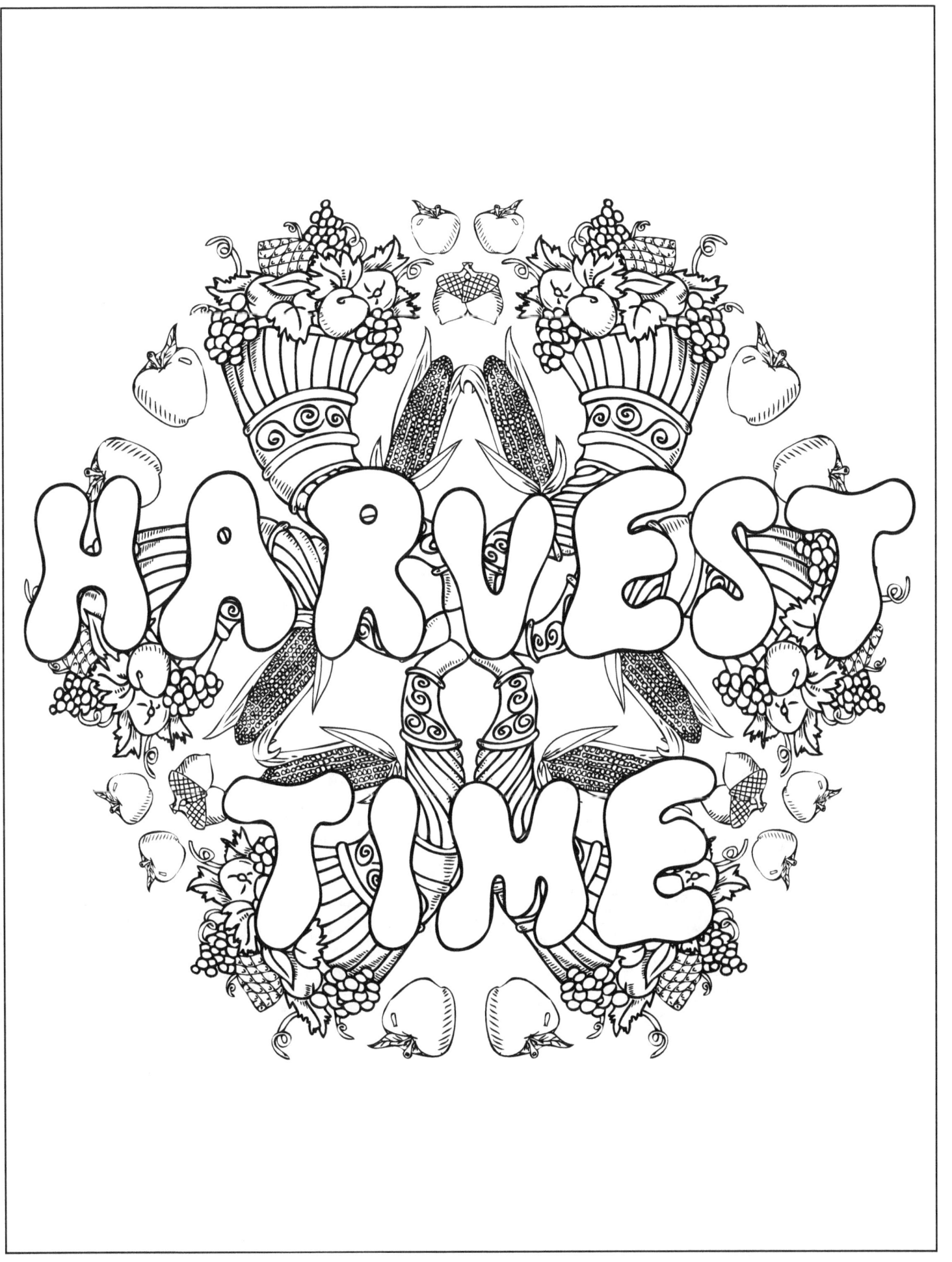

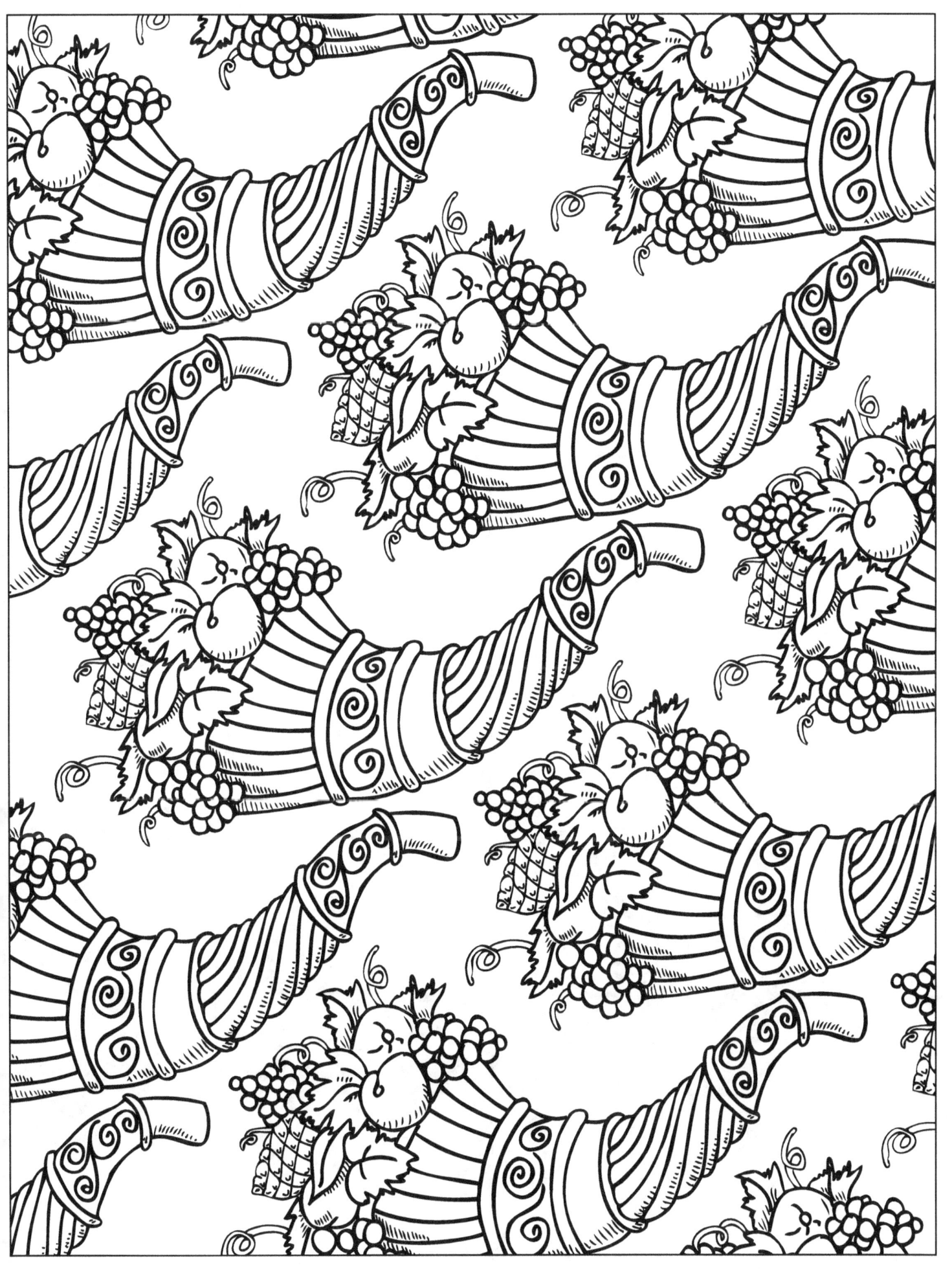

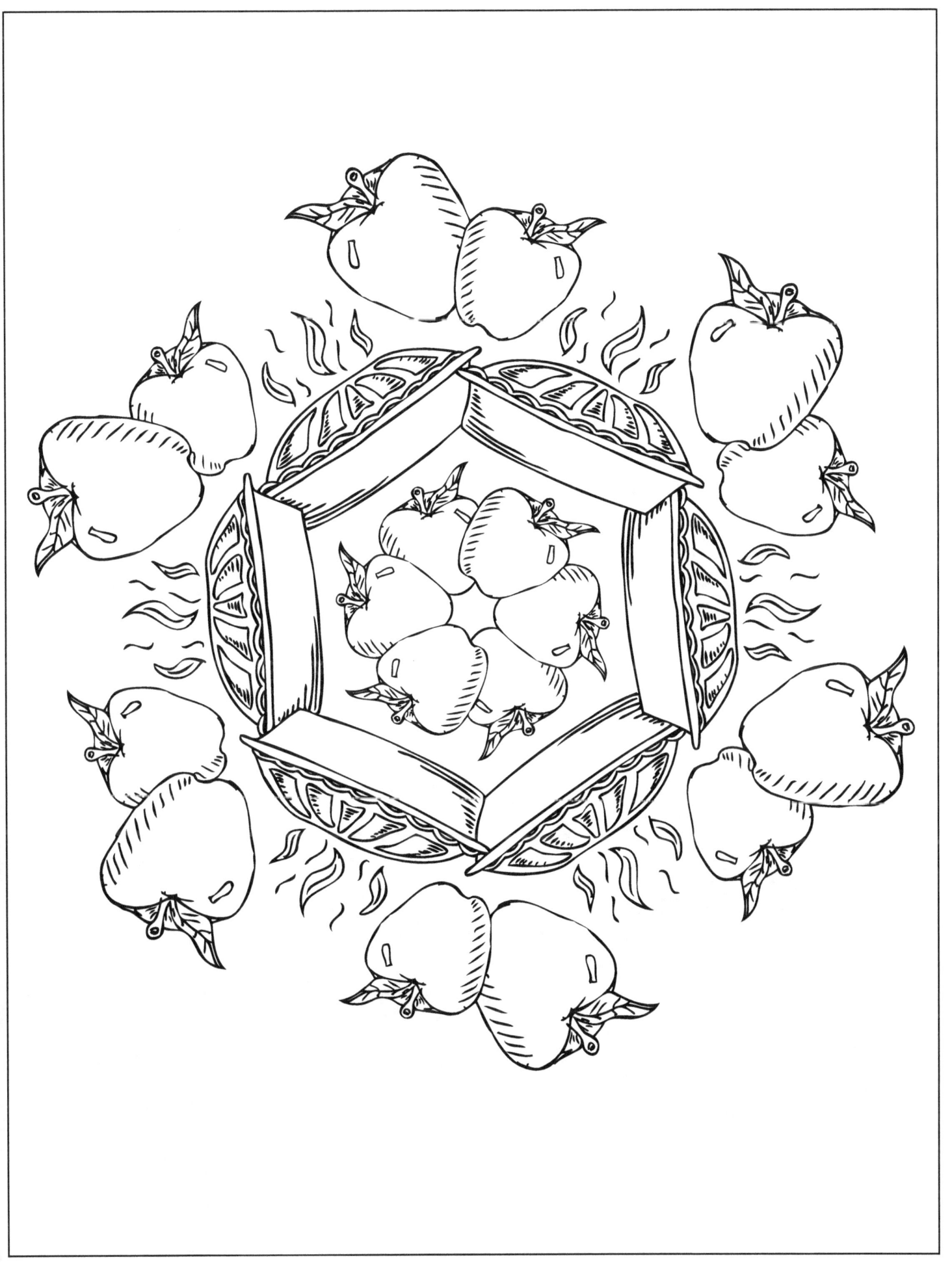

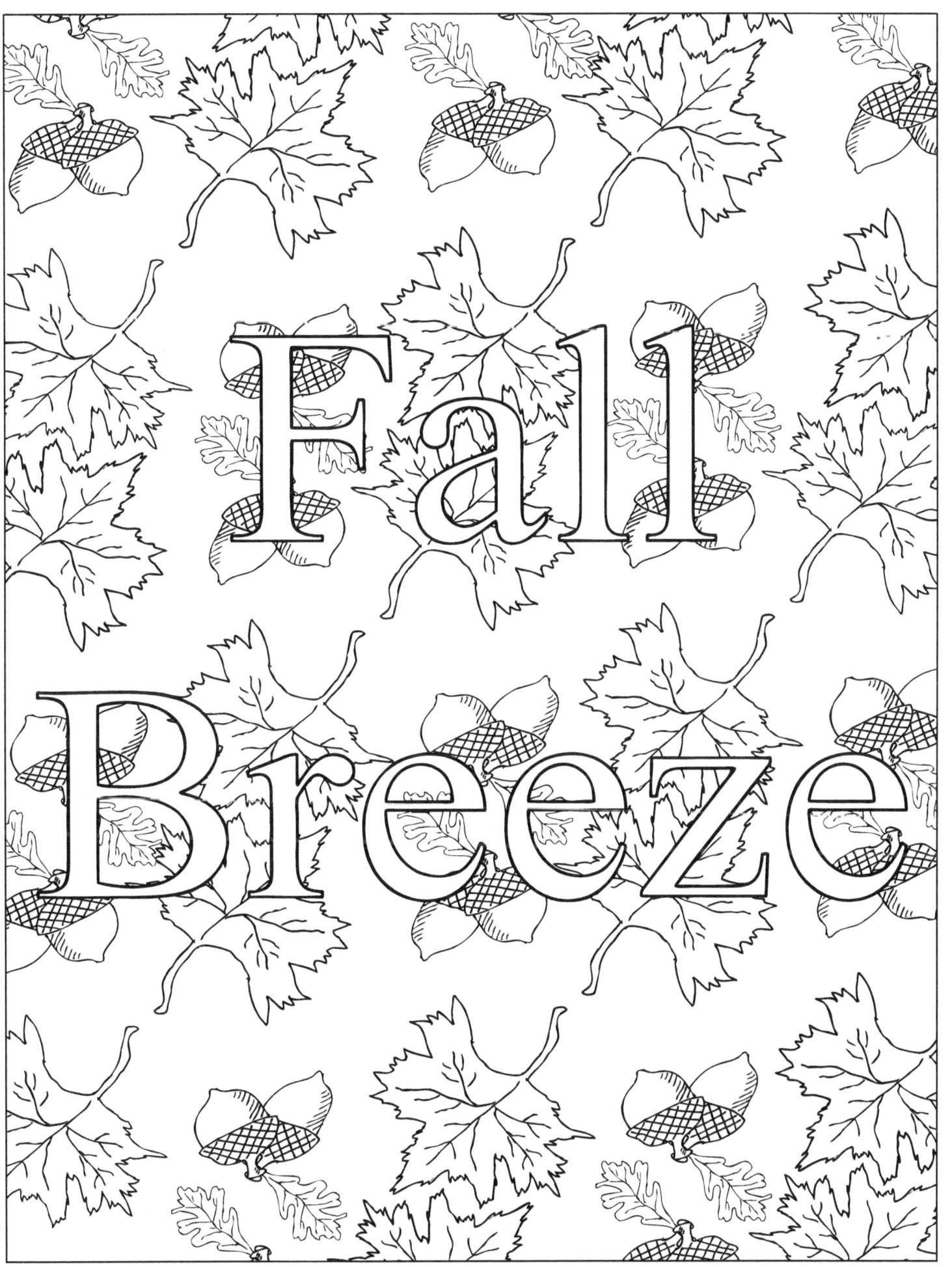

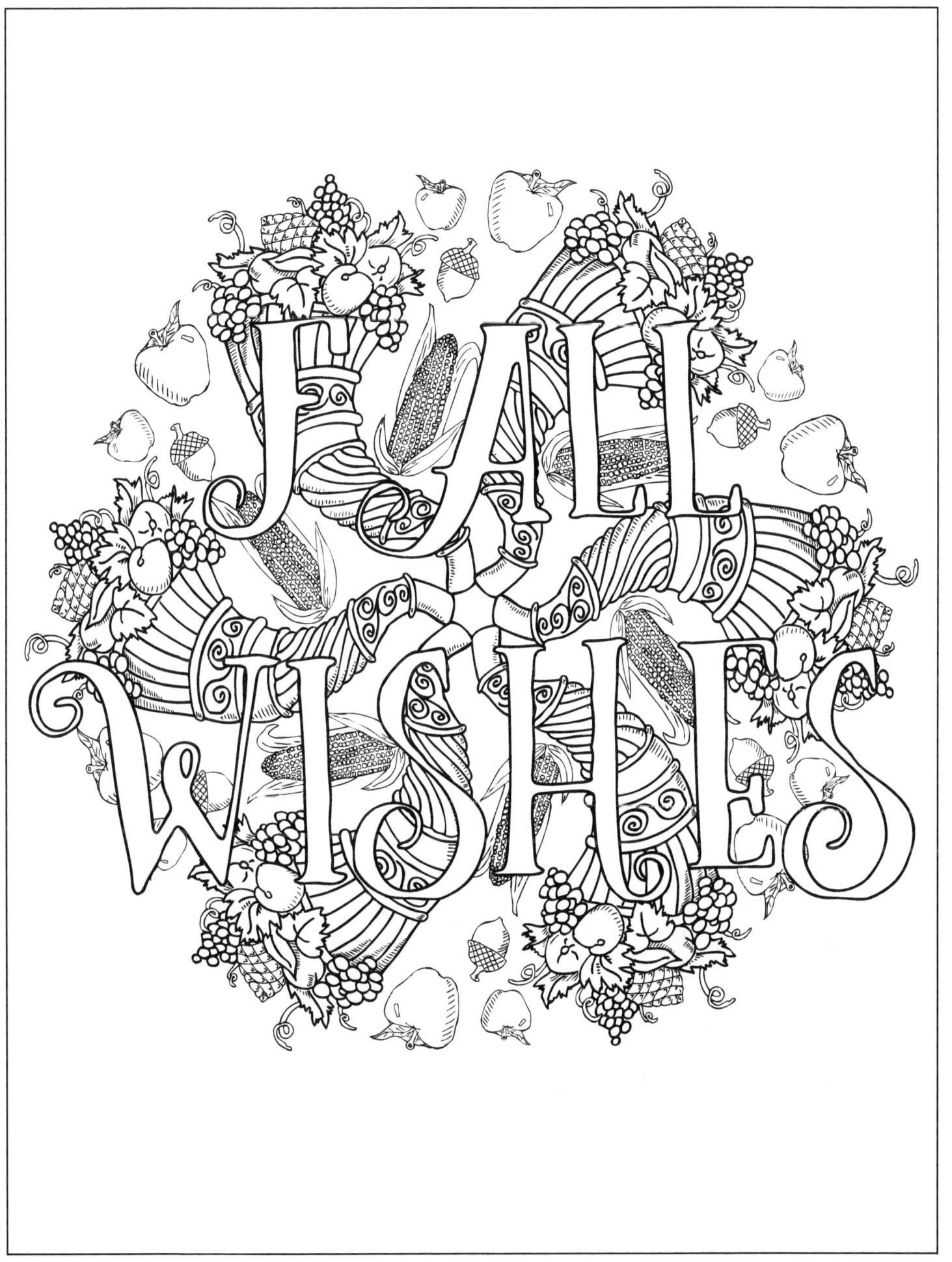

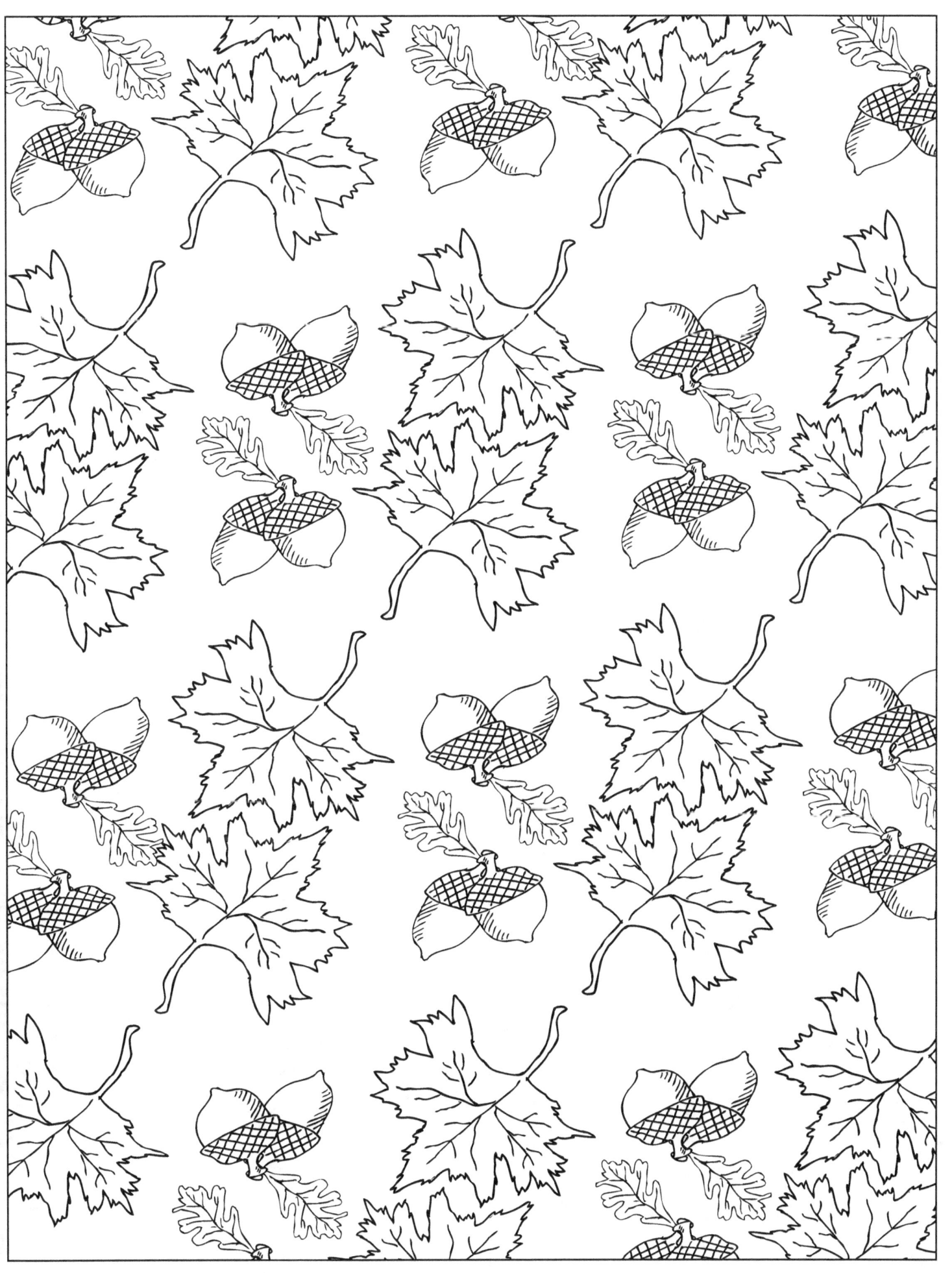

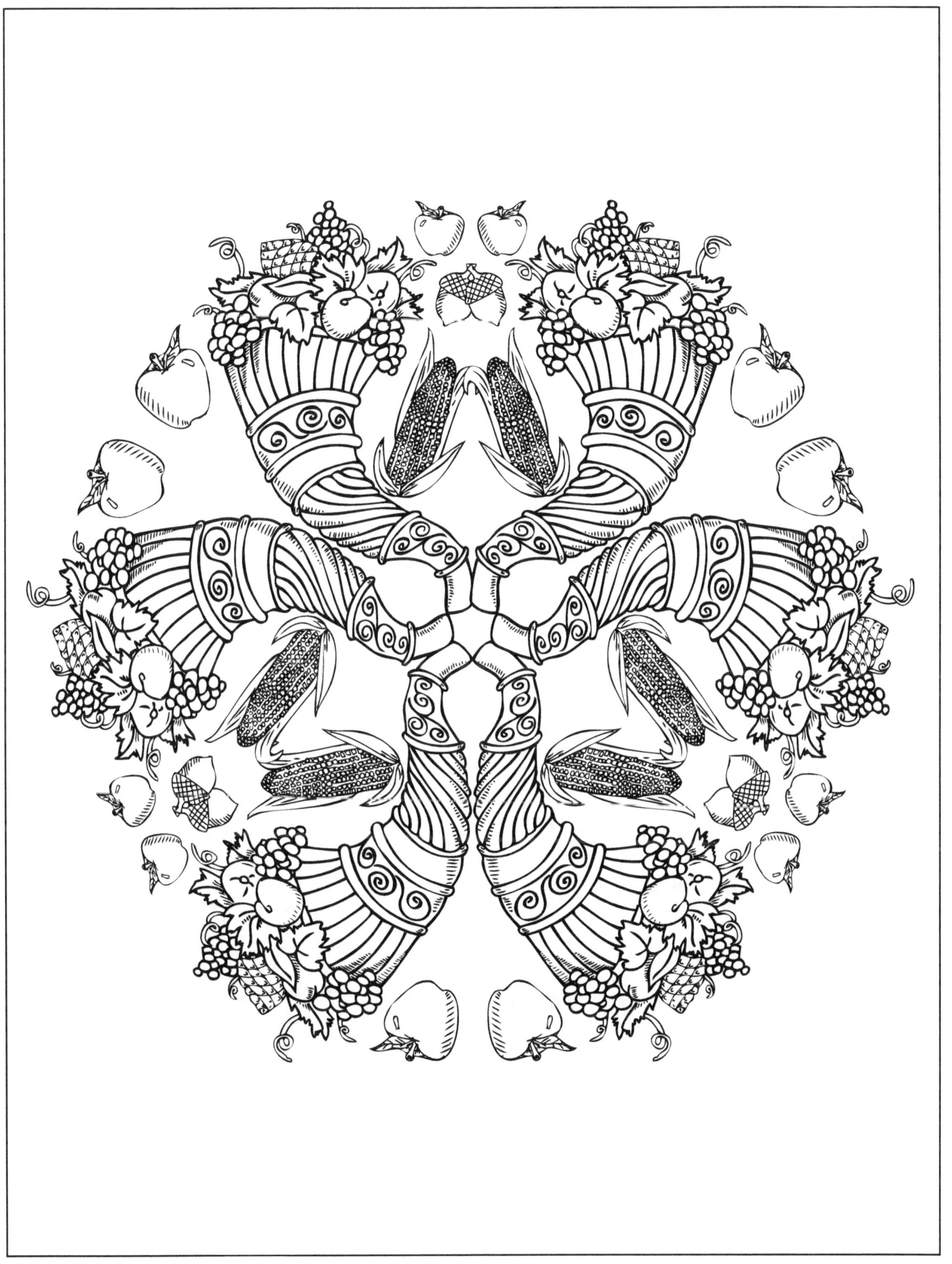

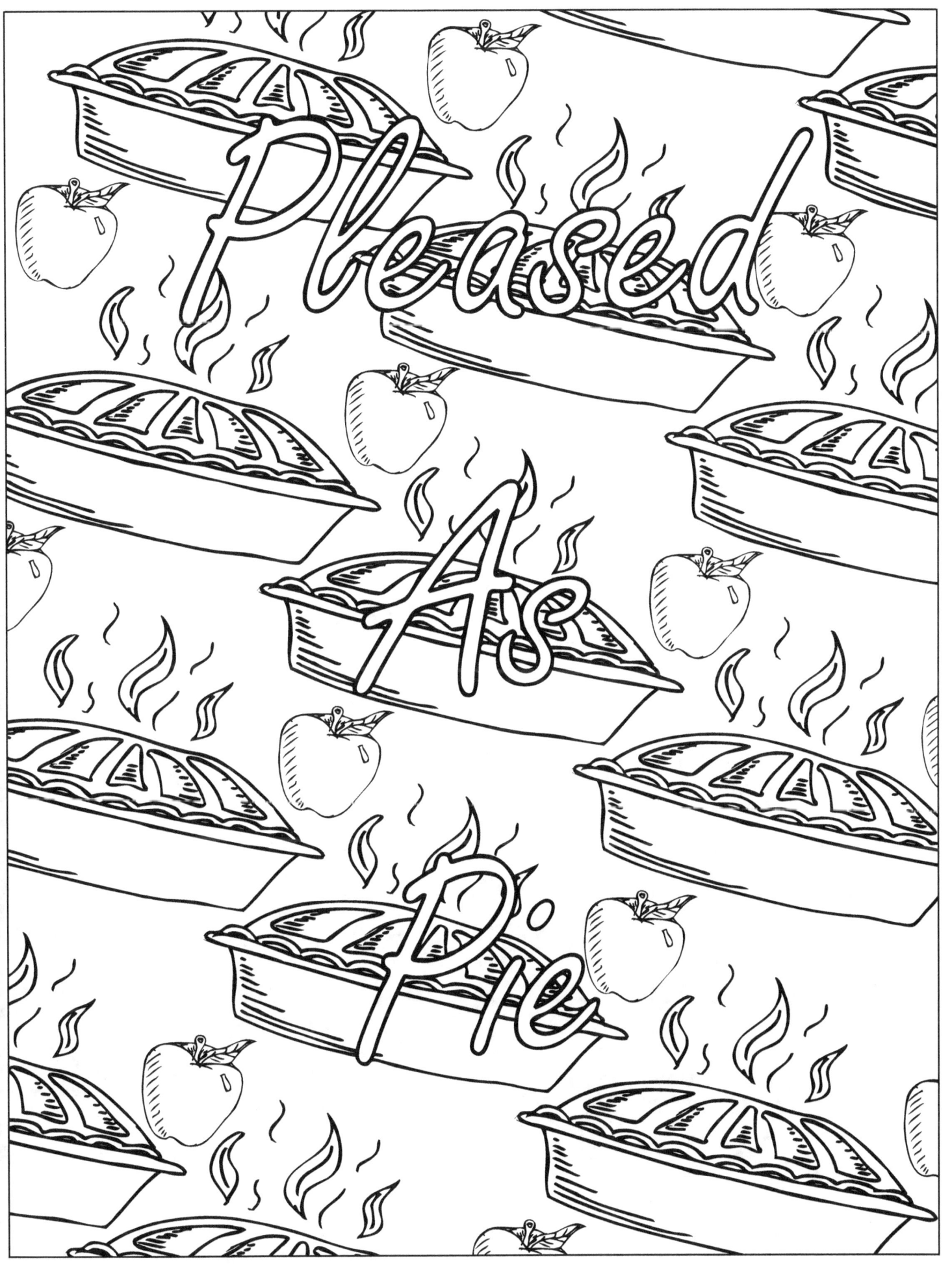

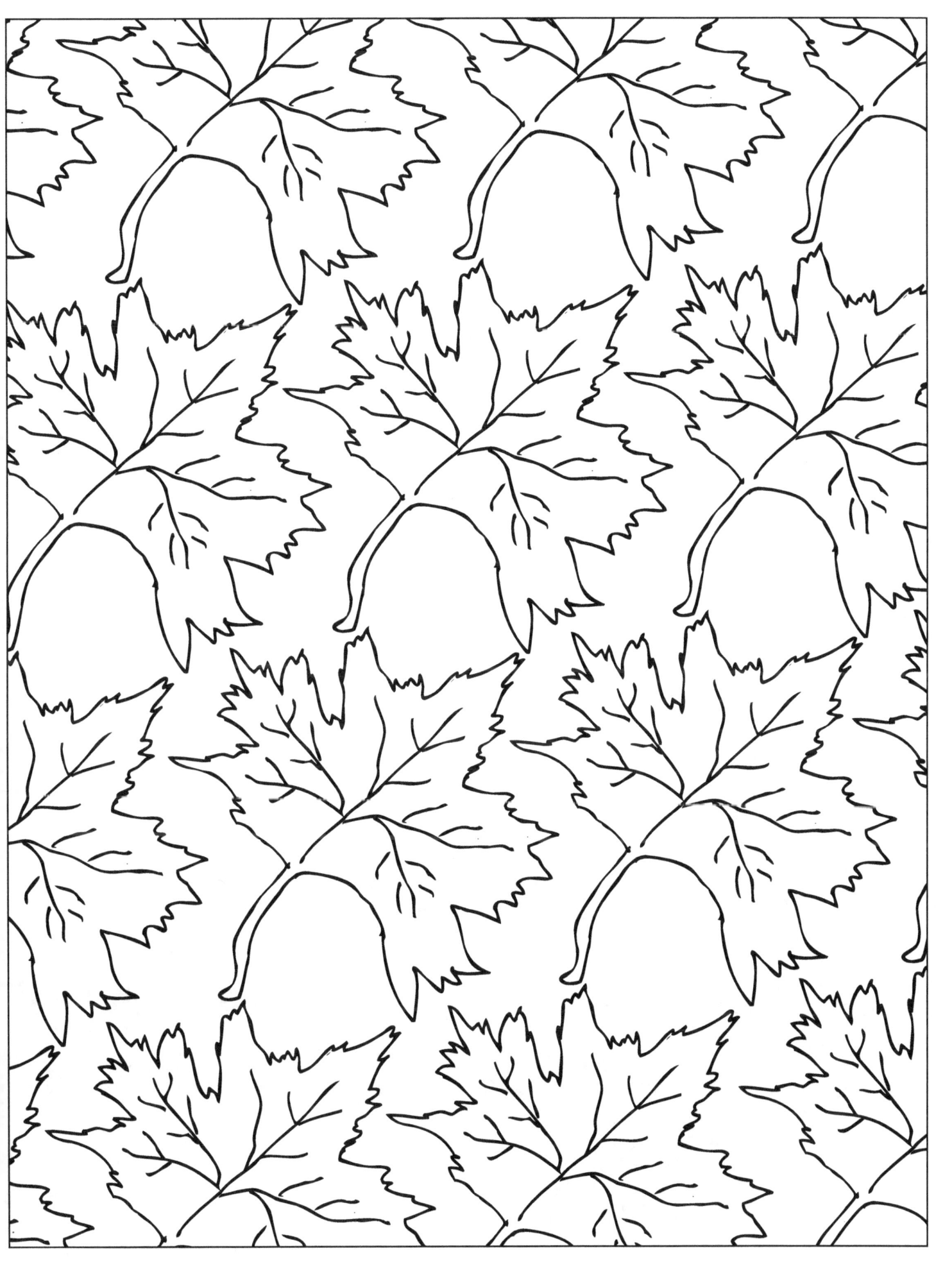

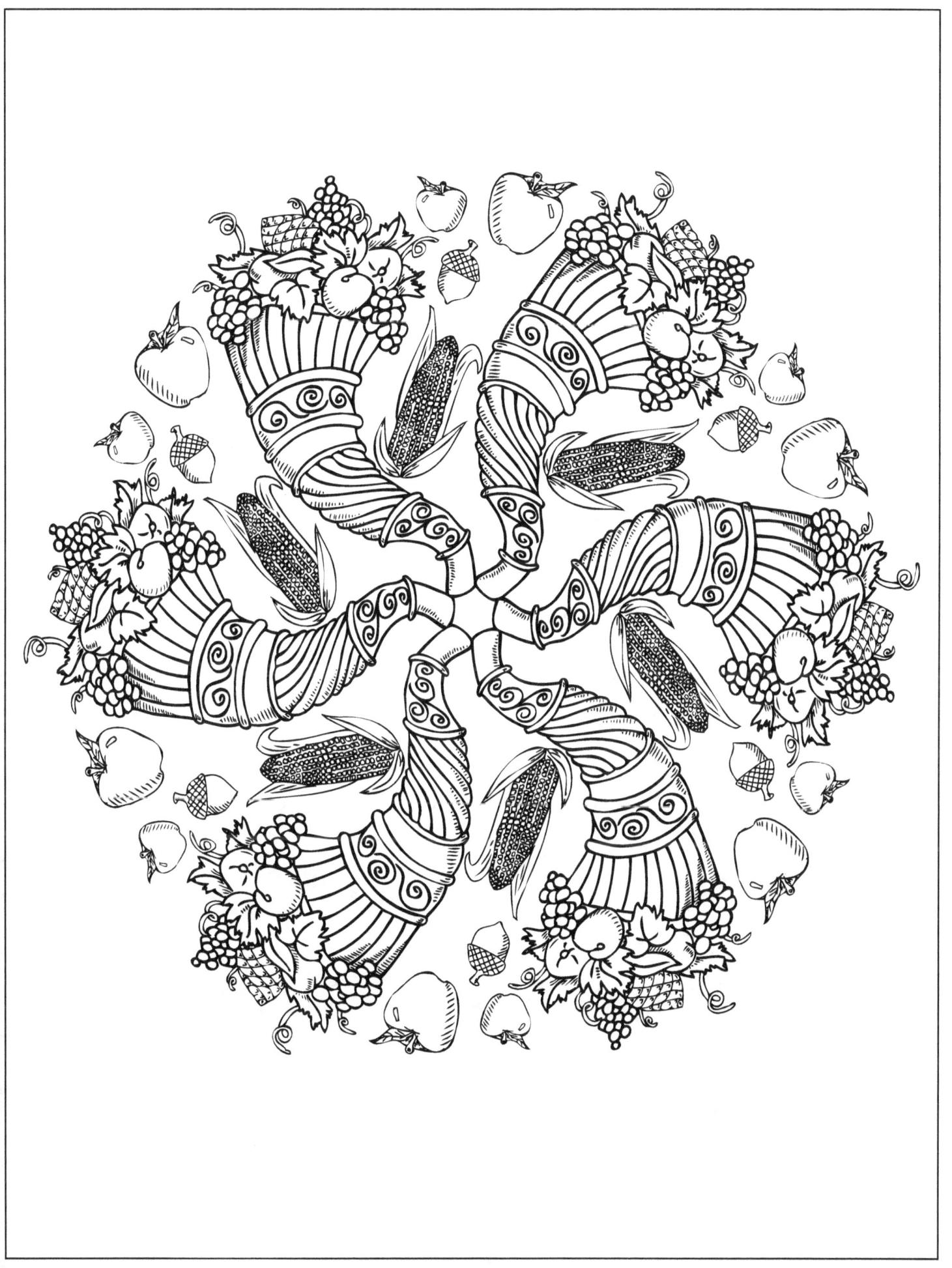

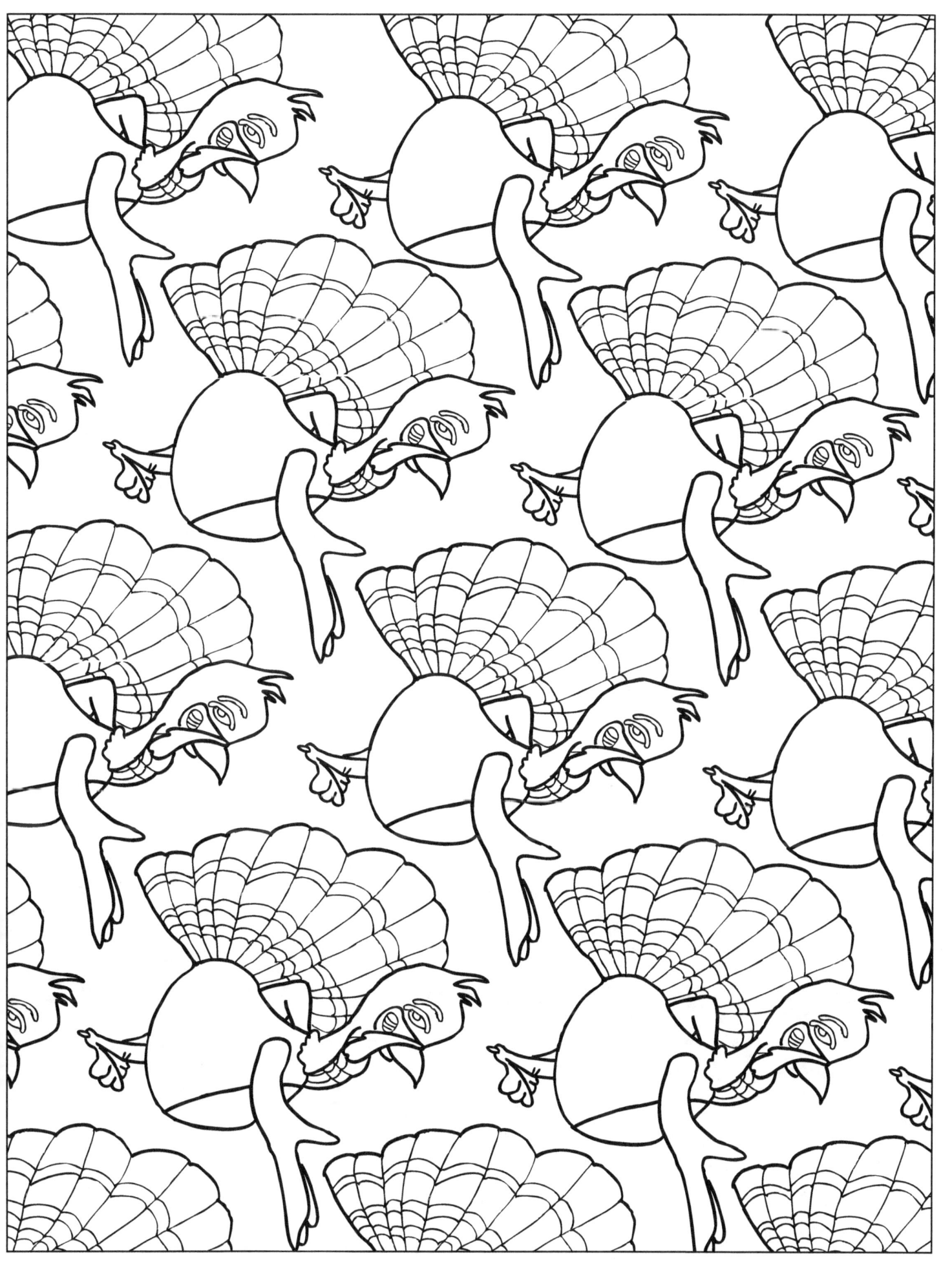

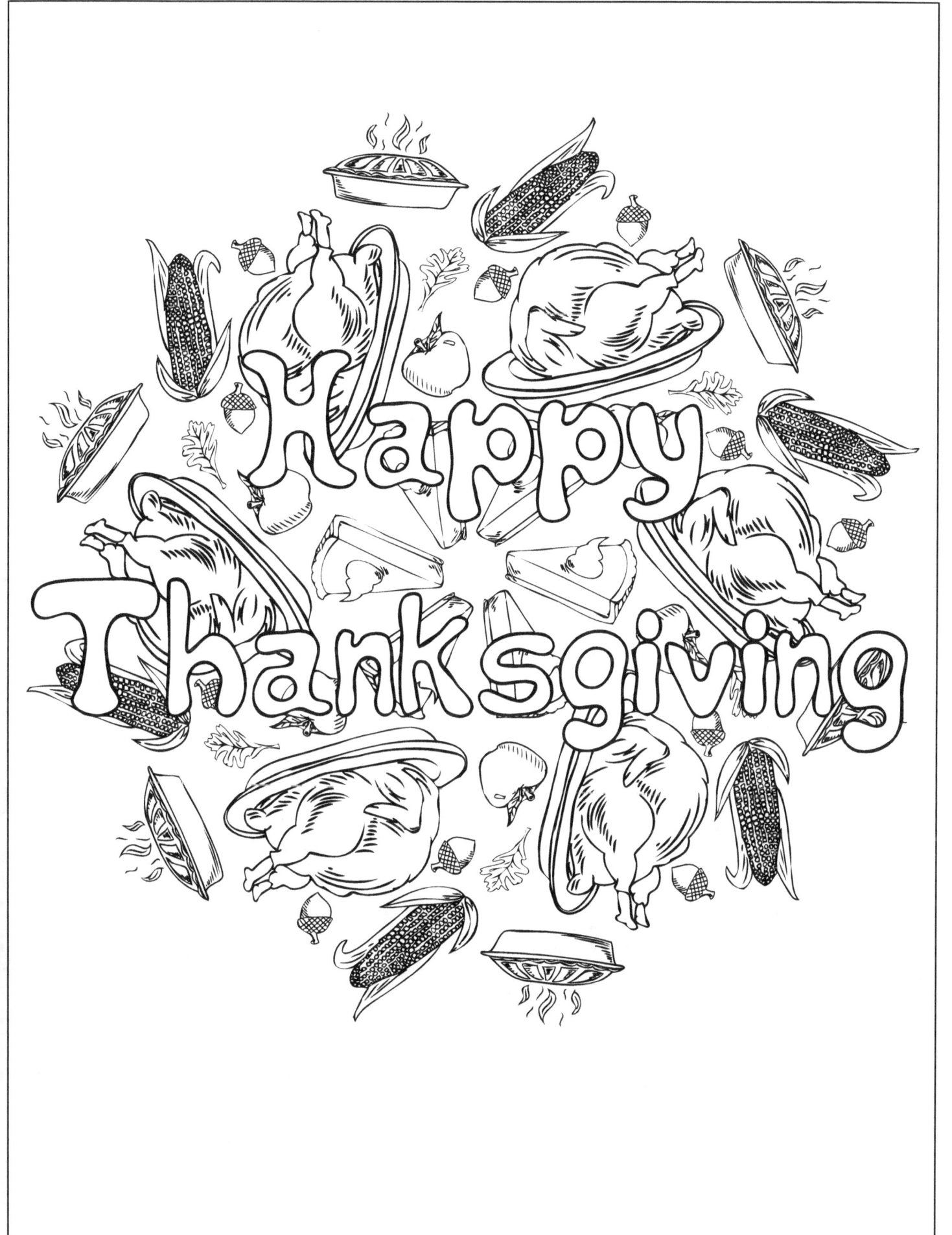

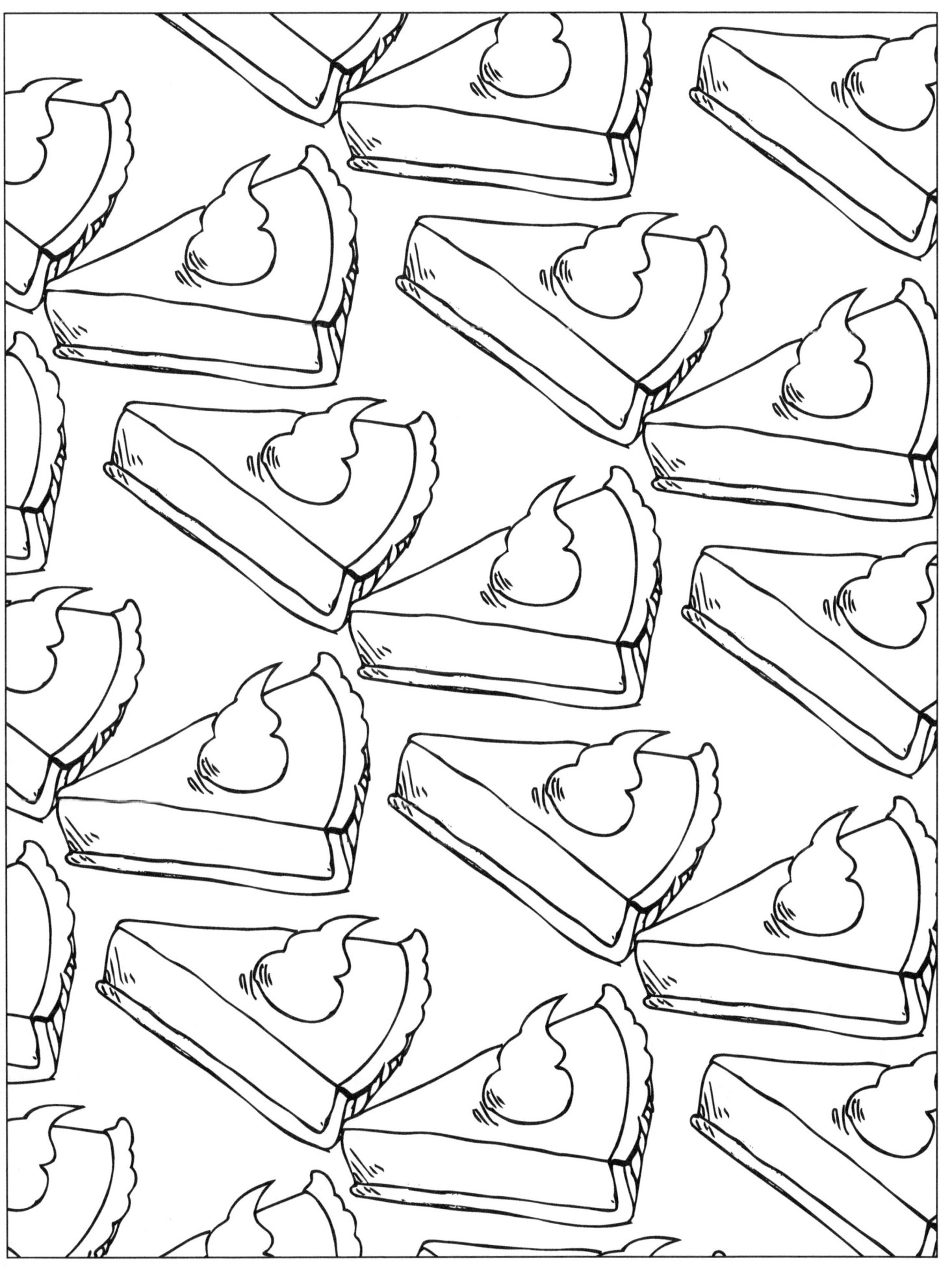

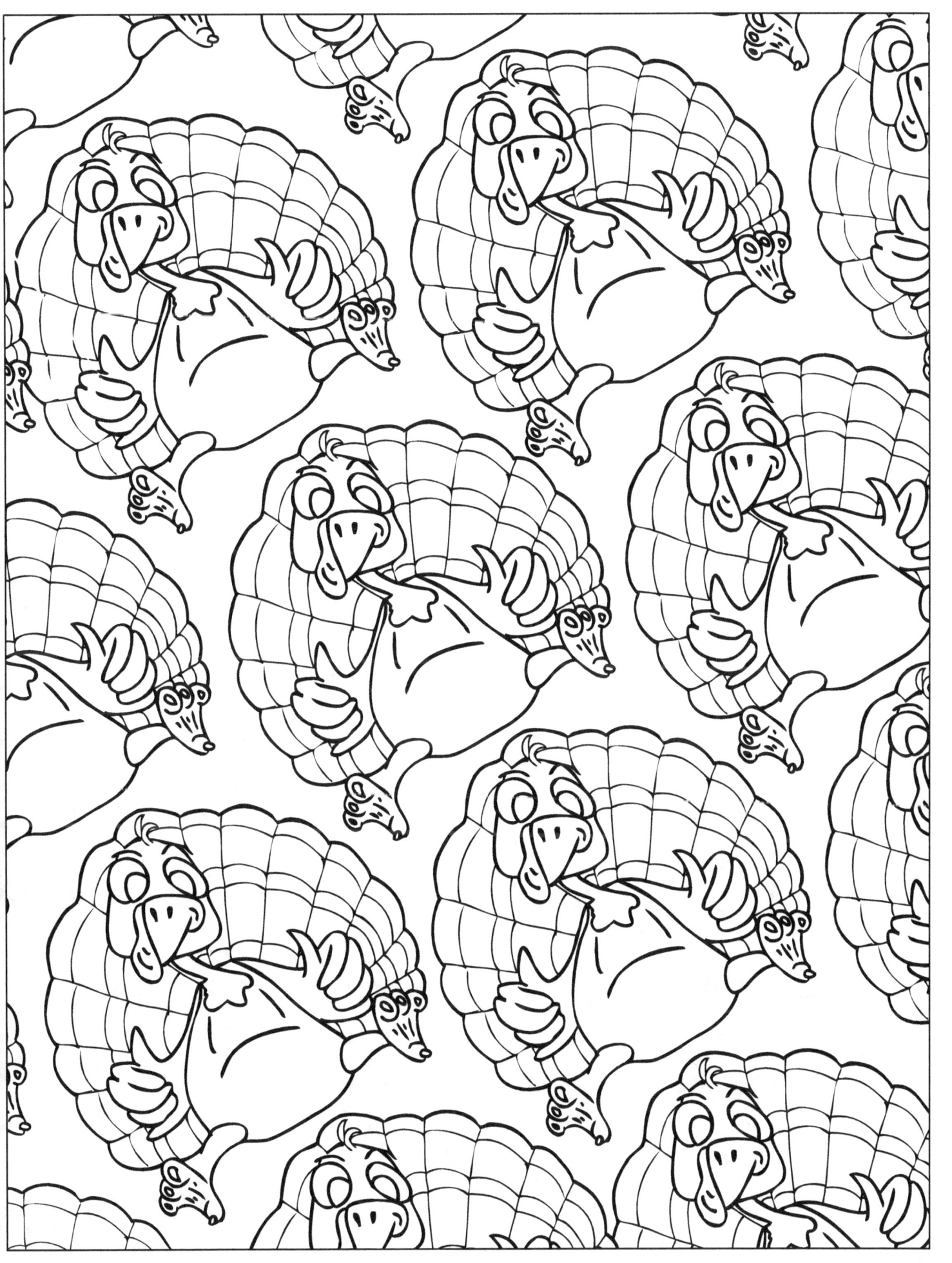

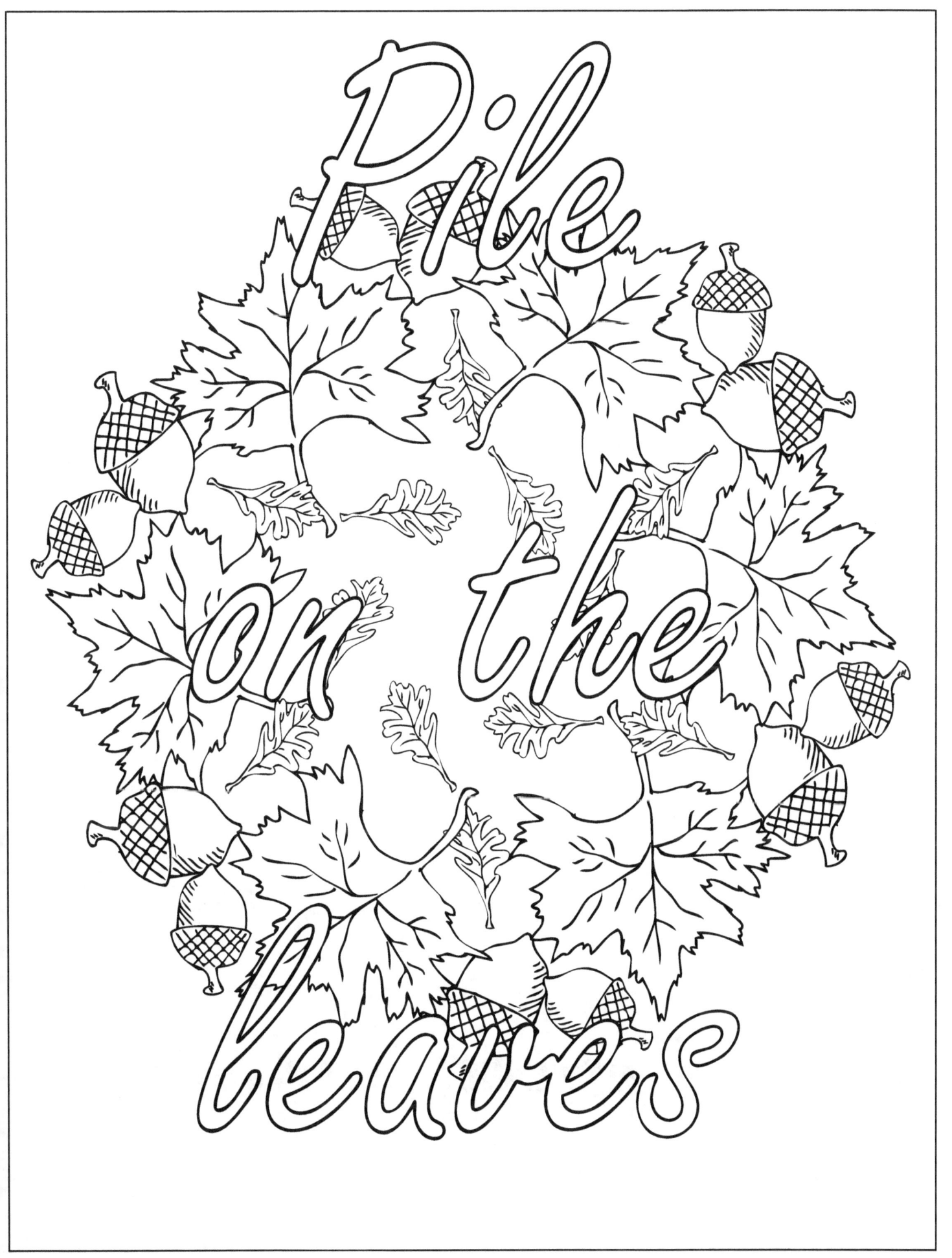

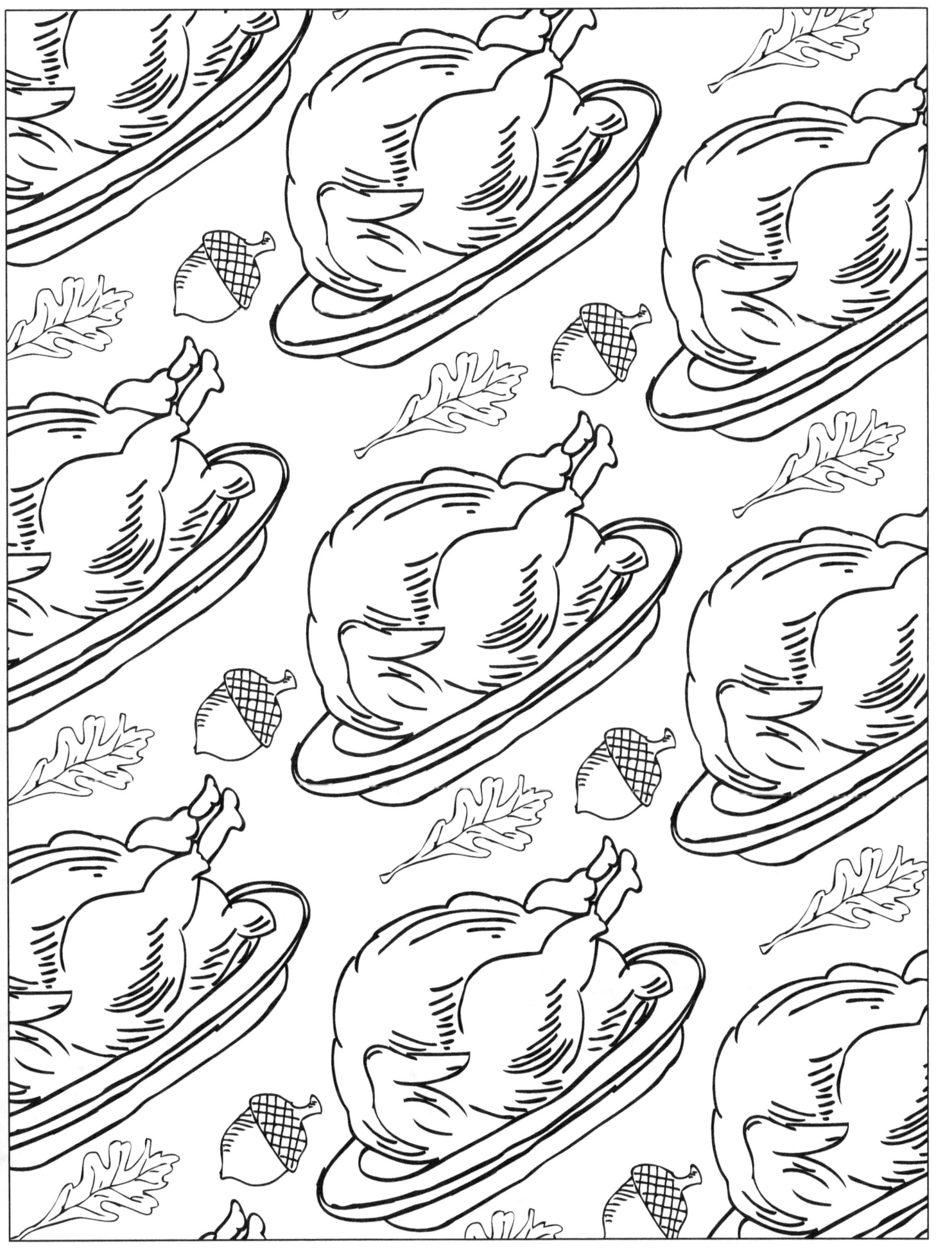

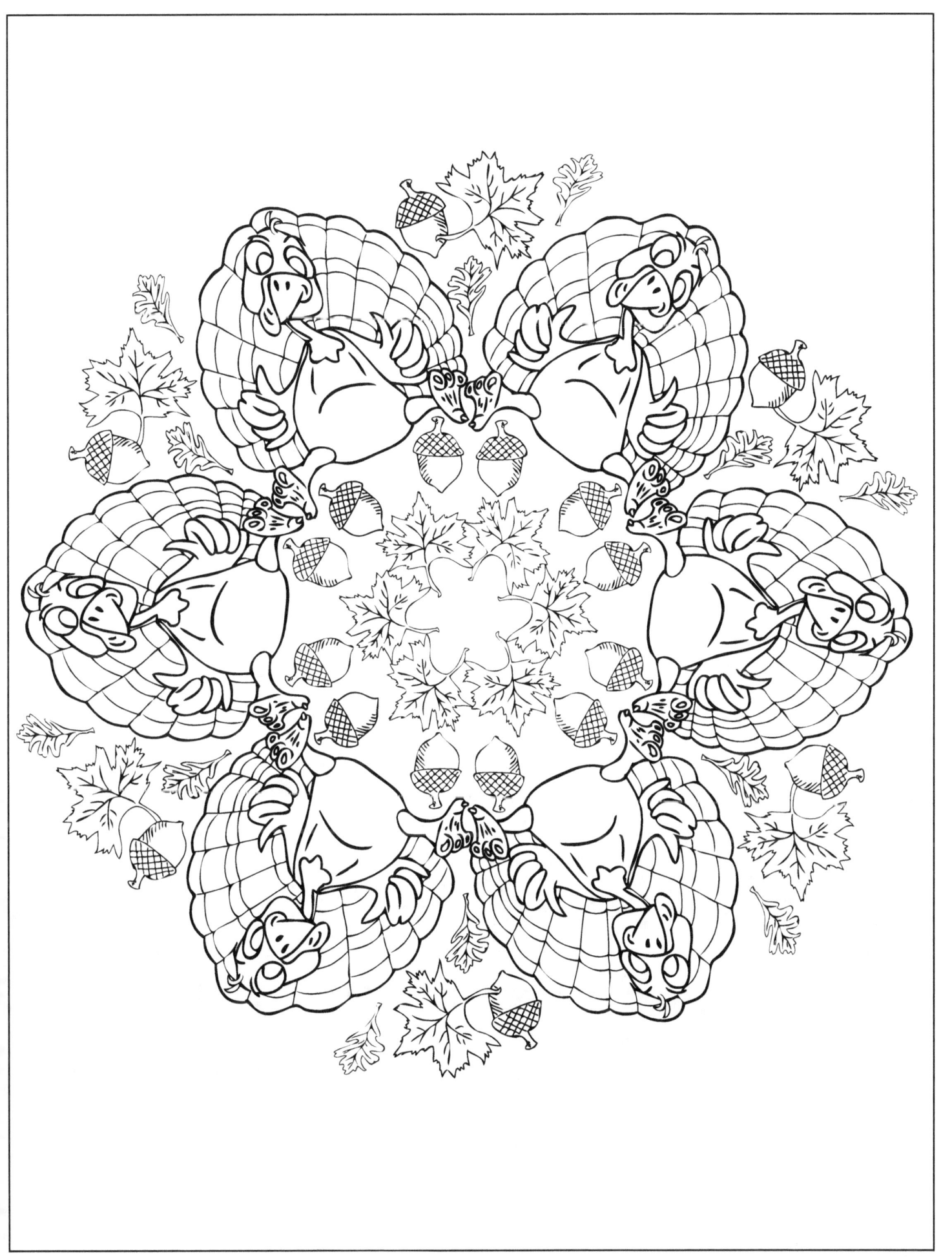

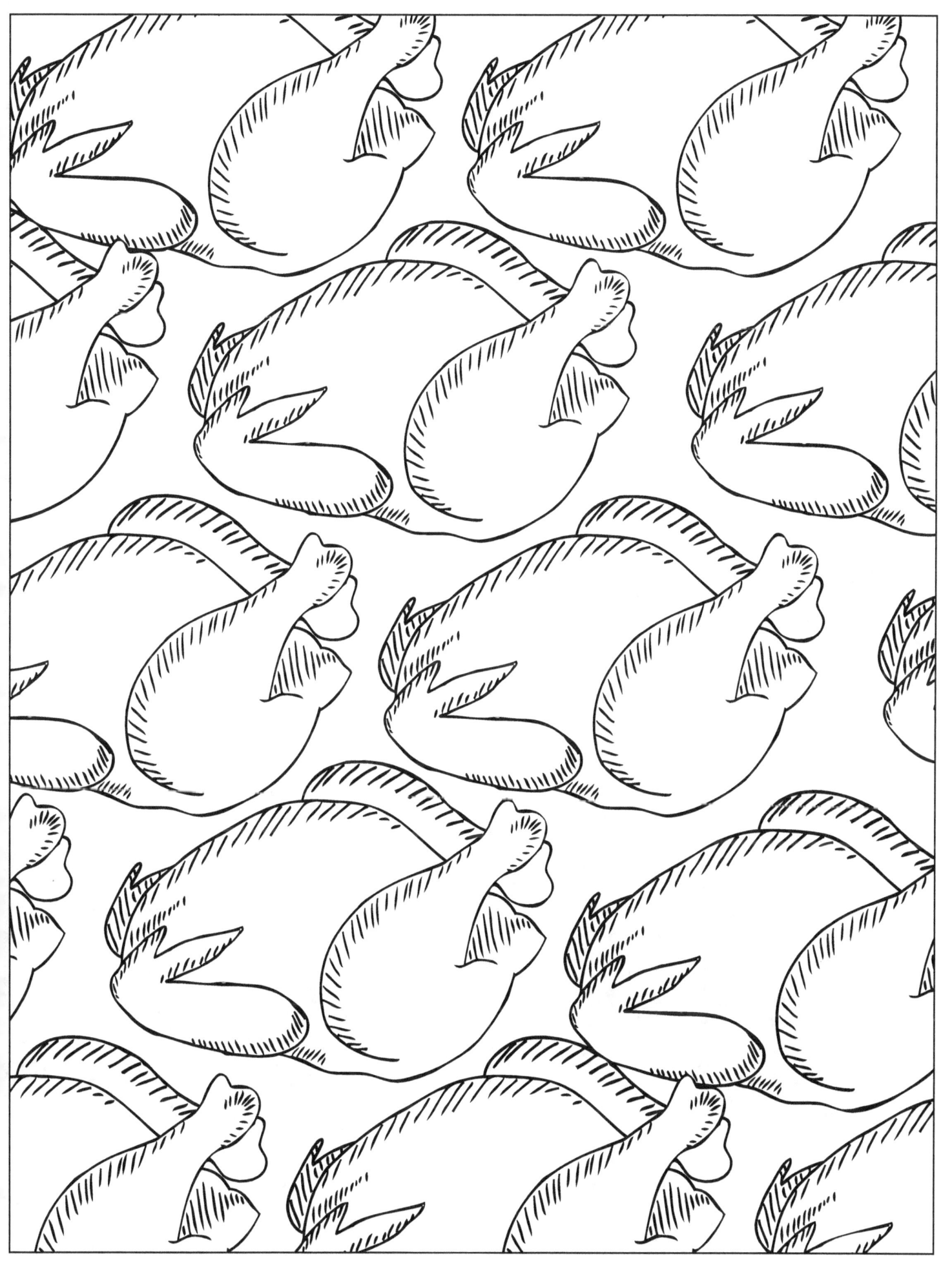

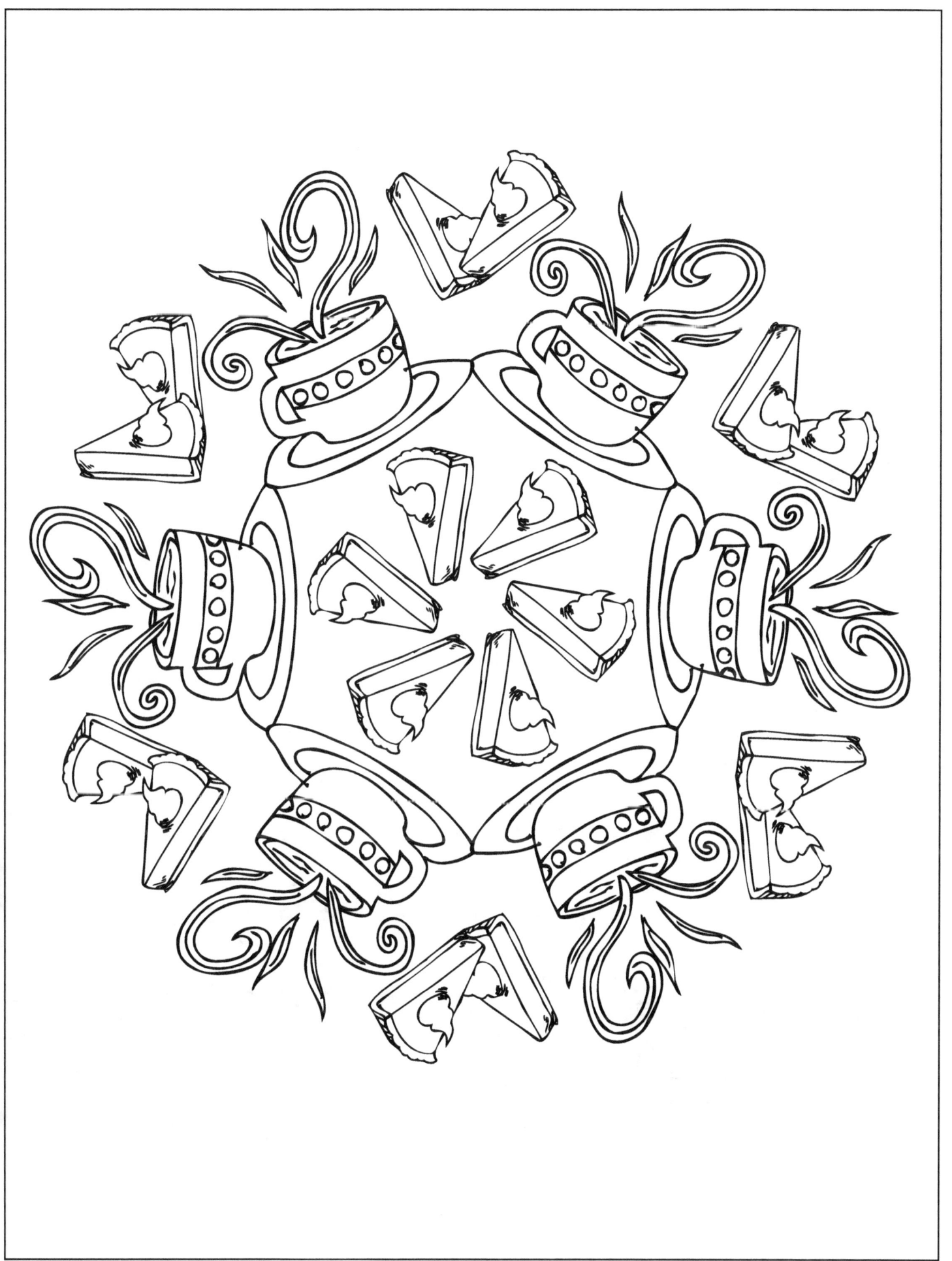